"Home"
Is Where
The Heart Is

By
Berneth Noble McKercher

To John Smith & family
especially. Enjoy
my book!
Berneth Noble McKercher

See p. 141

Published 1995
Printed in the United States of America

Dedication

This is the story about interesting people I have met and experiences I have encountered during two years of residing at Independence Village in East Lansing, Michigan (1992-1994).

I call it my "happy book" because it is the result of constantly having an optimistic approach to what retirement living should be all about. It is not meant to "sugar coat" any situation. Neither is it intended as advice for anyone who might not see things as I do.

All persons described within these pages have given unconditional authorization for the use of this information about their personal lives. However, there *is* one chapter in which I have taken the liberty to simply pay tribute to others who have influenced my life in very subtle ways.

To *all* the people who have contributed to this writing accomplishment, I shall forever be indebted!

Berneth Noble McKercher

Prayer of a Writer

Lord of all things, whose wondrous gifts to man
Include the shining symbols known as words,
Grant that I may use their mighty power
Only for good. Help me to pass on
Small fragments of Your wisdom, truth, and love.
Teach me to touch the unseen, lonely heart
With laughter, or the quick release of tears.
Let me portray the courage that endures
Defiant in the face of pain or death;
The kindness and gentleness of those
Who fight against the anger of the world;
The beauty hidden in the smallest things;
The mystery, the wonder of it all...
Open my ears, my eyes; unlock my heart.
Speak through me, Lord, if it be Your will. Amen

A Touch of Wonder
by Arthur Gordon

Submitted by Pauline Corzine (cousin) because it reminded her
of the author, Berneth Noble McKercher, as she pursues
her writing career.

Table of Contents

Dear Hearts and Gentle People

The time has come for me to announce that, as of October 1, 1992, I shall be residing in my new apartment in Independence Village. It is one of the newest of retirement complexes in the Lansing area and is absolutely *beautiful*.

This has not been a rash decision – just a healthy realization that I want to make this move while I am in good health and can make my own decisions. Although I have been blessed with good health for 77 years, it is best to be prepared for the time when I might need to slow down a bit.

I have been thinking about this for as far back as October 1990, when I moved to Raleigh House apartments where I have spent a comfortable and rewarding two years. I would recommend these apartments to anyone who needs comfortable and scenic surroundings with superior management and who is not yet in need of a retirement situation which offers complete security and adequate emergency assistance.

I am happy to report to you that my writing is showing great promise and that, with the aid of my family, I will have a productively efficient word processor office in part of a large bedroom. It will be much easier, in my new location, to pursue my writing career on a more active basis because of the freedom from housekeeping chores. It also means sitting down to a table for nourishing meals served in a warm atmosphere of friendly people.

I have visited Independence Village several times and am fortunate that I already know some of the residents well. One person, Anita, has played an important role in encouraging me to make the move because she was my neighbor at Raleigh House and we have become close friends. My aim is to be as well accepted as she has been – but I realize that much of that depends on *my* attitude and behavior.

I am definitely a "people person" and am happiest when I can have some of my peers around me. I also recognize the need for scheduling time for my writing and for keeping up contacts with many of the people who have continued to be a vital part of my life.

I have eaten at Independence Village and have shown my new apartment to most of my family. The food is *good* and the friendliness is even better!

I have long been a fervent believer that "Happiness is a state of mind" and that everything constructive that we do is mostly a case of mind over matter: winning out. It has ruled my life thus far and I intend to see that it continues to do so.

Along with this attitude, I have inherited a beautiful sense of humor which sees me through any rough times that come my way. I had not quite realized the extent of this until recently, when one of by bridge playing friends said to me, "I was so glad to get back to the bridge table after my vacation because I missed Berneth's funnies."

I have an extremely supportive family who understands my need for independence, yet they recognize how much I need their input with wise suggestions and emotional and physical support. I have accepted some slight nudges from them when making this decision; I have also accepted some slight tugs at the other end of the line by people who, apparently, are very anxious for my arrival.

To the people, in all walks of life, I am especially grateful for making my life so *great.*

I have led a very colorful life and I intend to keep it that way as I continue with my writing career and with my social life in the East Lansing area.

This story, which I have now written, will be included either as a special segment of a book which I intend to write or as a contribution to a syndicated column which is a possible accomplishment in the near future.

May God bless each and every one of you who have made and will continue to make this possible for me.

Angel on My Shoulder

Although I have never subscribed to the fatalistic or superstitious outlook, I must confess that there have been times when I have come perilously close to doing so.

Case in point.

Since moving to Independence Village, I recently experienced a ten-day series of events which reminded me of a very special uncle who was a funeral director (known as undertaker in those days). He often told me that whenever he received a body in his funeral parlor, he could almost always expect to receive another two within a matter of days.

Because of a series of events which could have been tragedies recently, I have thought of that uncle often.

Within a ten-day period of time in the month of November, I took a terrible spill at the entrance of St. Casmir's Catholic Church where I had planned to join friends at the bridge table. It has become an annual event to sponsor this special fund raising day and I was excited about it.

I remember sliding into the doorway, in a very un-ladylike position, and being thankful that I was wearing clothing which would not become too disarrayed. I also remembered to say, "Don't touch me until I can make certain that I am not hurt."

No doubt past recollections of seeing my beloved Mac on the ground after being injured in a community softball game conjured up his verbal warning to a well-meaning group of bystanders who were trying to help him. As he reached for his glasses, which were on the ground beside him, he realized that his arm was paralyzed, at least for the moment. He asked that no one touch him until the doctor arrived. It may have saved his life.

During my accident at the church I soon realized that, because I had no blurred vision or headache, I was free to get up from the ground.

While being assisted by a very fine young man who came running from out of nowhere, I entered the church to join my friends. I even was able to laugh when, later, a friend at another table said to me, "You probably didn't get hurt because you landed on your head!"

Just a few days later as I was traveling to my home in the Village in a blinding rain storm, I struck a median and blew a tire!

I was, literally, praying for help when along came a car which stopped to offer help. The driver was Rocky Beckett of Lansing.

I am writing a book about the good people I meet and it continues to amaze me that I seem to have an affinity for locating them.

Instinctively, I sensed that I could trust Rocky even enough to get out of my car when he offered to let me sit in his while he moved mine to the side of the road, out of traffic. Once he spoke to me I had absolutely no fear.

While waiting in my locked automobile Rocky returned to his home to phone for help, first offering me the choice of sitting there or going with him. It never once occurred to me not to trust him, so I remained at the scene while watching for a tow truck.

As he changed to dry clothing Rocky's wife, Julie, had assumed the responsibility of locating a service station which could send a truck. It was not an easy task because of the miserable driving condition.

Four days later was Thanksgiving and, as I prepared to travel to Kalamazoo to be with family, I lost a tooth – a very expensive one!

As usual, we had a delightful family day and, as I kissed my son farewell, I whispered to him that I felt certain I had left my tooth in Kalamazoo.

This now accounts for the three "almost disasters" within a short period of time. I remember feeling a warm glow as I entered the lobby of our complex and realized how safe I was in such an environment where people really cared about my safety.

While talking with staff members at the front desk, I learned that our manager had also experienced triple events which were pretty frightening. His wife had recently undergone multiple by-pass heart surgery; his father had experienced major surgery; when driving home from the hospital, our manager struck a deer and severely damaged his automobile – all within a matter of days.

My semi-fatalistic approach is closely related to a firm belief that things will eventually come out right. Too many times has this happened for me to consider it coincidental.

In fact, as I write this chapter for my book, I have experienced two great sadnesses over which I have no control and I keep wondering what will be the third – before a very special happiness takes over – *because it always does.*

In all of these accidental experiences that have happened, there has been the constantly glowing feeling that God has placed a very special angel on my shoulder.

I have telephoned Rocky Beckett to tell him so and that he has been the inspiration for this chapter of the book which I plan to call *"Home" Is Where The Heart Is.*

Judge Not a Book by Its Cover

"Men resemble the gods in nothing so much as in doing good to their fellow creatures."
– Cicero

Shortly after meeting Bus and Betty Robertson I remember first thinking that they appeared to be so completely "whole" that I wondered why they had moved to Independence Village rather than remaining in their own private home. It did not take me long to understand the answer to my question, *"why?"*

On the surface this couple seemed to be so self-reliant that there surely was no need to depend on others for sustenance, almost to the extent that, on occasion, I confess to wanting to call their bluff!

Within a matter days I began to realize that Bus was so in control of his physical limitation of "legal blindness" that I refused to consider this a handicap. It did not take long to realize that his wife, Betty, had the beautiful gift of making this *happen* for her husband. She seems to have a gift of knowing when he needs her support, yet she also respects his need to do as much as he can for himself. He assumes this role in a modest way that makes one realize that there is not one shred of self-pity in this very fine man.

When Betty says, "Bus will be all right as long as he has me," I know that she means that he also needs the backdrop of good friends which he will continue to find in Independence Village.

I understand this situation well because I often have someone come up to me with the remark, "What are you doing *here?*" At times, it bothers me that I have to explain that I came here because I *wanted* to – while I could make rational decisions and could "navigate on my own power" as long as is humanly possible.

Living here has taught me more compassion than I had ever thought possible. It has also brought me the comfort of knowing that if I should be incapacitated there will be people who really care. Because of this, seeing people who appear to be less fortunate than I (physically) has only taught me to say a silent prayer for them – *often*. It is these people who have taught me more than I could ever learn from a book, believe me.

Whenever good deeds are being passed out, expect to see Bus and Betty Robertson just around the corner for they seem to have an uncanny sense of when these services are needed. This shows up in their genuine hospitality toward newcomers; in their volunteering of services at special activities; in Betty's clever suggestions, such as in her "Did You Know?" contribution to the Village Spotlight News.

"When the roll is called up yonder" it is the people like Bus and Betty Robertson who will be sitting in the front row! I intend to find many others who qualify for my book *"Home" Is Where the Heart Is*. I am just as certain that time will not permit me to reach as many as I would like to.

It amazed me that Bus has signed up for gardening, which proves that he intends to do the most that he can do with limited eyesight. Although Betty does all of the driving of their automobile, I notice that Bus is out early enough to get the car started and warmed in cold weather. It was also he who helped *me* climb over a snow drift in order to reach my car which was parked in the carport and even waited to make certain that the engine has started.

It is not my intention to embarrass these fine people in any way by making them a part of my book. It is simply that I need their contribution to the book which I hope will tell my story about living in a retirement village.

When I hear such comments as, "Sparrow Hospital has taken over Independence Village," I bristle because in my heart I say another silent prayer because I am so thankful that many of these people can experience good care in dignity.

Our Miz Liz

There is an old expression that "first impressions are the most enduring." *Not so!*

Elizabeth (Liz) is the first resident that I met on the day of arrival at Independence Village and it was she who taught me a very dear lesson in humility. For even as I recognized a pronounced display of efficiency as she stood behind the front desk, I also felt a secret sense of bewilderment as I wondered how a resident could have so much authority.

I did not know for several days that her courtesies at the front desk were strictly voluntary. In fact, to this day, occasionally someone asks me whether I think that Liz was paid for her gracious assistance at the desk.

I am assuming that very few people can understand *why* anyone would give such dedicated service without being monetarily compensated for it. It is something which I have always understood and been able to accept, but this time it forced me to make my first apology to a resident living at Independence Village. I was astounded at how easily the words "I'm sorry" came to my lips as I confronted Liz personally, simply because I needed her to accept me.

There have been times when it has been difficult for me to accept an apology because I felt that I needed to "beg the question." Any apology which has to be asked for is simply not worth my time.

Not so with Liz, who, without hesitation, accepted my words of contrition and even told me that I had "made her day." It is a day which I never shall forget because it was the beginning of a beautiful friendship.

Elizabeth Lamphere was born in Owosso, Michigan, and moved to Alberta, Canada, at the tender age of one. Her father died during her fourteenth year and she moved with her mother and a sister to Ovid, Michigan, where she lived until graduating from high school. Her brother served in the Australian navy during her childhood.

While residing in Lansing, she attended and graduated from Acme Business College where she also worked for doctors. During these years she married H. Wayne Lamphere and continued working until her beloved Carol Jean was born.

When Carol Jean was in junior high school Liz went to work at Kellogg Center as a receptionist whose expertise involved the registration of conferees attending conferences. I may even have attended some of those very conferences.

Because names of people have always fascinated me, I found it interesting that "Liz" became the nickname for my new friend whose name is Elizabeth. Probably this is because I have other friends with that name but this is the first "Liz" in my life. The others were either "Beth" – "Betty" – or "Bess."

I know of only one person who calls her "Elizabeth" and he tells me that that was the name which he had read either on her door or on the roster of names in the lobby. As I pass her door several times a day, I sometimes chuckle at how the names of Liz Taylor and Liz Claiborne often come to mind. One of them because of beauty; the other because of style. My "Liz" possesses both of these!

Because we have met so many times at the large mirror on the wall as we turn the corner of our hallway, we now smile as we pass. Both of us think that it is an excellent place to get a last-chance look before we enter the lobby or the dining room. It has reminded me, also, of how often I met John Phillips at that spot and how he called me "pretty lady" as I called him "handsome dude." He is no longer with us at Independence Village and I truly miss him – mostly because of his bravery during a terminal illness.

As I observed Liz during her frequent appearances as a volunteer receptionist, I often marveled at her tact and poise at times when it would be understandable if she lost her patience – and showed it. Now that I know of her years of experience in doctors' offices and at Kellogg Center, I understand how this all has come about. It has also reminded me of how much I have learned about the residents after talking with them and often learning just "how they tick." Time will not allow me to do as much of this as I would like.

We have so much in common as we move from table to table in order to greet more people; as we abhor constant complaints; as we have learned true compassion for others who may be less fortunate than we.

I now understand that, before I arrived at the village, no wheel chairs were allowed in the dining room. It is, indeed, a good thing that I was not living here when this happened and I am glad for the recognition of the evils of discrimination.

For several years before moving to Independence Village, Liz resided at *The Chateau* apartments. It is ironical that I considered a move to these apartments at the time of the sale of my Okemos home, but at the time there was no vacancy. I believe that destiny led us to each other. Or, as a younger person once said to me, "It has become my Karma." I simply love adding this word to my vocabulary.

We have shared many experiences through visiting with each other; through moving from table to table in order to better understand more people; through learning to forgive. Perhaps we can also better learn how to forget by continuing to share our common concerns. Not long ago, I was accused of being a hypocrite because I did not always forgive. This is probably true and Liz has helped me realize that there are some things we simply cannot change – especially attitudes. When I have explained to her that I often ask God to forgive another person but that I also need to ask Him to teach me to forget, she has understood.

We have shared many humorous experiences which have kept us on an even keel while dealing with our lives. We have also felt free to discuss possible solutions to problems – much of it through compassion. We have learned that we can not always find a solution and must simply walk away.

There is a humorous experience which I have come across since getting acquainted with Liz, but she will not be aware of it until she reads it in this chapter.

Because I know of her intense love for cats, I have from time to time sent her a card with one or two on the cover and have recommended a special cat calendar which she decided to purchase. One of the cards was cut out in the exact shape of a cat and was so realistic in appearance that several people have told me that they wanted to pet it as they saw it on the wall near the apartment door.

The punch line here is that *I have always hated cats!!*

Quiet Courage

"Don't cry out so loud
that you can't hear opportunity knock."

Submitted by Bob Hall

Almost daily, as I read this refrigerator motto," I am reminded of my frequent visits with Robert (Bob) Hall who also is a resident at Independence Village.

After occasionally interviewing more flamboyant personalities, I became almost riveted on observing someone who has *almost* escaped my eye because of his calm and quiet acceptance of life's problems.

Bob Hall is just such a man!

He was born on September 8, 1915, in Oil City, Pennsylvania, and spent most of his youth in that city, graduating from Oil City High School where he also began his career as a tool and die maker. He pursued this work at Westinghouse and Active Industries where he also became a purchasing agent for stampings for all major automobile companies.

He moved to Kalamazoo, Michigan, where he attended classes at Western Michigan College before it became Michigan State University and, later, a member of the "Big Ten."

I can also recall that MY school was once called Michigan Agricultural College and that recently some friends of mine in Swartz Creek, Michigan, gave me one of the original glass milk bottles with an M.A.C. embossment which they had found buried in their back yard. There also is a street on campus named "M.A.C.", but many people now call it "Mac Avenue."

Bob Hall married Margaret Boling, who preceded him in death on September 24, 1993. This marriage had been enriched by the birth of three boys, the three D's – Dick, Donald and Dennis. Bob served in the military services for a period of four years, three and one-half of them in the States where Margaret could always be with him. From there he was transferred to the Philippines and Japan. In fact, his was one of the first troops to enter Japan in WWII.

After the war Bob and his family lived in Pigeon, Michigan, and it was from this village that he and Margaret moved to East Lansing and were one of the first couples to enter Independence Village. Here they were able to enjoy being together for some of their "golden years" until Margaret suffered a severe stroke and was transferred to Whitehills Health Care Center.

It was at this time that I first met Bob and my life has been made richer by having visited with him many times in our lovely lobby as he awaited transportation to and from the nursing home. I often noticed how impeccably dressed he was, in a quiet and unassuming way, with his black shoes shining to perfection!

Bob walked with a cane but he managed to make the necessary trips to our beautiful dining room and to his first floor apartment. In fact, he made the move to a second apartment on the first floor and was not completely settled when news came of Margaret's demise.

He handled himself throughout his many travails in a "manly way" (words from by grandmother) and only occasionally did I see tears in his eyes. Whenever he became aware that I was observing this he would say, "I am really just fine. The only sorrow I really have in my life is my beloved Margaret." It was then that his eyes actually *glistened* and he seemed even a bit embarrassed that I would catch him.

Bob sat regularly at a dining table which I needed to pass in order to reach my own and I made it a policy to stop and ask him how he was doing. It was then I recognized a dry sense of humor as he called me closer to say, "I didn't quite understand John Smith (also a resident) when he told me your name, so would you please write on this slip of paper?"

As often happens, when I wrote the name "Berneth" I felt it was necessary to pronounce it and to explain that it is the first half of my mother's name (Berthia) and the last half of my father's (Kenneth). To this day we often laugh because one time Bob calls me "Berneth" and the next day it becomes "Bertha."

It has reminded me that my mother spent an entire lifetime trying to convince people that her name actually was *"Berthia"* and I have most of my life explaining that I am not a *"Mr."* To this day I frequently get mail, or even an occasional check, addressed to *"Mr."*

There is a sentimental side to the personality of Bob Hall that tells me he would like me to include the very special poem which was imprinted in the memorial card during Margaret's funeral.

The Rose
It is only a tiny rosebush –
A flower of God's design;
But I cannot unfold the petals
With these clumsy hands of mine.

The secret of unfolding flowers
Is not known to such as I –
The flower God opens so sweetly
In my hand would fold and die.

If I cannot unfold a rosebud
This flower of God's design
Then how can I think I have wisdom
To unfold this life of mine?

So I'll trust in Him for his leading,
Each moment of every day,
And I'll look to Him for his guidance
Each step of the pilgrim way.

For the pathway that lies before me
My Heavenly Father knows –
I'll trust Him to unfold the moments
Just as he unfolds the rose.

I have learned *so much* from this kindly mannered man! I have also discovered a very special sense of humor which, even in troubled times, has been able to utter these words to me at a time when I was a little impatient with people.

"The screw that is loose in one's head is also the one that holds his tongue in place."

May God continue to bless this fine man and his family!

Special note: As I complete the writing of *"Home" Is Where The Heart Is,* I am now seated at the dining table with Bob Hall. He tells me that he sometimes wants to remind me that he doesn't have much to contribute because he is "just a farmer." Of course, he has spent much of his life away from the farm, but we never forget our roots.

Little does he know that it was the *FARMERS* who often kept the food on our table as payment to my physician father. In fact, Dr. Kenneth Noble may have started the first hot lunch program in Michigan public schools. It was called the "Noble Experiment" and received national recognition.

From the littered desk of jolly ol' Harry M. Harris...

Speak to Me at Writing Speed

Good friends and good conversation have always been a joy. Today, good conversation has become a lost art.

I can no longer enjoy good conversation, because in the aging process my hearing, amongst other things, has degenerated and I cannot hear most speech at the normal speed. The hearing aides do not help much.

I am tired of asking people to repeat what they said, I alibi myself by thinking that if I haven't heard it in all these many years, it isn't worth hearing.

Often when people talk to me I just nod my head and try to look attentive. I even put in an occasional "yes" when I think it belongs.

I will even turn down an invitation to a group, because I will not be able to join in the conversation.

So, if you talk a bit slower I may be able to hear you. Therefore, please speak to me at writing speed. ♥

*Retirement Village Extends Independence

Now that I have resided for several months at Independence Village in East Lansing, Michigan, the time has come for me to address some of the misconceptions about moving into a retirement village. From the day that I made this decision to this very moment of writing, there has been no doubt about the wisdom of having made such a decision.

Fortunately, I have a very supportive family, emotionally and physically, and they recognize my need to remain as independent as possible. So the transition was a smooth one, with a minimum of anxiety.

Friends and relatives were informed via a letter titled "Dear Hearts and Gentle People." Almost without exception, these people were supportive in their reaction and I settled in to becoming a very "Happy Camper."

Unfortunately, I have discovered a few disturbing myths (misconceptions) concerning a transition from private housing to a retirement center and I hope to prove them wrong so that some of my peers will consider or reconsider.

I need to speak from personal experiences here at Independence Village because this is wherein lies my credibility.

I did visit several such residential situations and would advise others to do the same before making a final decision.

I have friends living at Burcham Hills and Delta Retirement Centers who are just as happy with their decision as I am with mine. The choice becomes a very personal one which only *you* can make – if at all possible.

If you have ever considered making such a change, there are perhaps a few things which I might advise for you:

1. You should make this transition while being as independent as possible. For many, this includes being able to continue driving a car for awhile.

2. Choice of locality should be one where you can also continue some of the activities which you have always had. For me, this meant East Lansing.

3. You need to look for the advantages of "safety valves" such as emergency pull cords and railing guards; health protection; accessibility to dining room (preferably a lovely one) which provides nutritious meals.

4. Understand the advantages of eating those meals with the companionship of others who "speak your language."

5. Be aware that there will be grumblers and groaners such as you will find in *any* society, but that *you* can make a difference.

6. Realize that any kindness or cheerfulness which you extend will be returned ten fold!

7. If/when you see wheelchairs, you will soon learn that some of those people have the sweetest dispositions.

8. If you appreciate management, management will appreciate you.

9. Keeping in touch with people who mean much to you is very important. At no time should you harbor even the slightest feeling of being out of touch with the world.

10. Making new friends, wherever you decide to live, is essential to comfortable living. However, living in the protective environment of a retirement village, you will be allowed to live as private a life as you wish.

Because I happen to be a "people person" it has been gratifying to know that I have access to the love of young people. Most of it I find right here. Some of it I continue to search for because it has always been a way of life for me.

My life has not changed all that much because I have the necessary space and time to pursue my writing.

You can be just as happy, providing you bring with you a positive attitude that life is for the living.

*Published in the *Lansing State Journal* (January 22, 1993).

It's Later Than You Think

"Procrastination is the thief of time."
– Dr. Young

As I have become more and more involved with the writing of this particular book, I am also more aware of the need for me to schedule my writing time more judiciously!

Shortly after learning of the demise of Bob Williams on May 19, 1993, I was abruptly awakened to the fact that I had planned to make him the next hero of a chapter for this book. This is a second reminder that I need to discipline myself to get my thoughts on paper while I can still *talk* with the person. "Tempus fugits" much too rapidly at times!

Fortunately, I had talked in bits and pieces with this very interesting man so that I can piece together what came across to me as a challenge to my writing.

Shortly after I arrived at Independence Village Bob was named as "resident of the month" and was crowned on his 99th birthday. I remember that he made a very fine speech about how much he appreciated the friendship which he had found while living here. I also got the impression that he hoped to make it to a very special 100 year celebration which many of us had hoped to provide for him.

Some people have disagreed with me when I have said that I wanted so very much for this to happen for him, mostly because they would, rightfully, not want him to continue the suffering which he was experiencing while in the hospital. They also would not want him to have to experience the indignities of residing in a nursing home. I would not want this for him either!

Yet, when one or two persons expressed the thought, "Why would *anyone* want to live to be 100?" I can relate to this attitude. Most of us, when facing a crisis or observing it happen for someone else, can sense what that person is experiencing. For anyone to want to reach the age of 100, or any specific age, it can be an unfulfilled accomplishment if it doesn't happen for them.

None of us would want this to be accompanied by suffering, yet we respect the individual's optimistic view about his own immortality. For me, it reminds me of my beloved father who passed away at age 69 which, in 1952 seemed *ancient* to me. Yet, even in the final weeks of his pain, he continued to hope to reach the age of 70 and to begin his fiftieth year in the practice of medicine. Not many men could come even close to accomplishing this and I respected my father for this.

I also was taught to administer the pain-killing morphine during his final moments and was glad that I had taken the time to inventory the number of babies which he had delivered into this world, including five of his own. When I reached the number of 3,000 babies he asked me to go no further. It was a tedious task which I feel very grateful to have accomplished.

Humorously, I recall how my father also said to me, "If I make it to the next election, I shall cast my very first vote for a *republican!*" The candidate's name was Dwight Eisenhower.

One of the most interesting tales which Bob Williams told me was that of his experiences with the Chatauqua tent shows in which he was a very active person. He seemed amazed that I know so much about these shows and that they remained such an important part of my heritage. I even remember that I may have been one of the few kids on the block who realized that she did not dare take the risk of crawling under the tent for free admission.

As we talked about his Chatauqua days, I detected a glint in his eye which only fond memories can provide.

It was then, too, that I realized a delightful sense of humor which was often displayed at the dining table where his lovely wife, Ruth, always managed to place him in as comfortable a position as possible. One time, I overheard him say that he usually chewed his food on one side of his mouth so that *all* of his teeth would not give out at the same time.

From time to time I was made aware of the depth of love which existed between this gracious couple. I think I may have witnessed the very best of it when Ruth returned to Independence Village following a stay in the hospital and we were so pleased to see her guiding Bob through the halls and onto the elevator.

During one of those times when I was talking to them, Bob said to me, "When Ruth returned from the hospital I got a new lease on life!"

I doubt if Bob even knew my name, but he did know that I am a writer and he knew that I intended to interview him for one of the chapters of the book which I am writing about Independence Village. I hope and pray that I have come close to telling how I felt about this very fine couple. ♥

"They Shall Have Music Wherever They Go"

"Music hath charm to soothe the savage beast,
To soften rocks, or bend a knotted oak.
I've read that things inanimate have moved,
And as with living souls have been inform'd
By magic numbers and persuasive sound."
— *Congreve*

Even before becoming a resident at Independence Village I was aware of the melodious tones coming from the piano and organ by Ellen Griffith and Thelma Geraldine Greeman.

At first there was a scheduled program which included dinner time music and Monday evening "Singalongs" in addition to occasional specials at such times as Christmas and St. Patrick's Day. Later their music schedule was slightly altered but residents continued to appreciate their unselfish efforts whenever they were comfortable about bringing their music to us.

Ellen's birthplace was in the Norwegian community of Elk Rapids, Michigan, and being the first grandchild gave her a feeling of being loved most devotedly. As I listened to her talk about Elk Rapids I could identify, for I spent much time in the Traverse area when visiting my sister at Torch Lake and when teaching summer classes for Michigan State University. It is truly "God's country" and I got to know many people in the area.

At the age of ten Ellen's family moved to Mancelona and she has always remembered their homes to be comfortable and spotless. The mother was the disciplinarian of the family and the father encouraged his children to love music, creative crafts and the sheer joy of reading together.

Even as a small child Ellen set her goals toward becoming a teacher. After graduating from high school she entered Augustana College in Rock Island, Illinois. Just as she was about to graduate she received an invitation from the President of the Board of Education to teach Music and Art in the Mancelona Public Schools. I identified with her as I learned that she, too, began her teaching at the tender age of nineteen.

She later completed her BA degree at MSC (now Michigan State University) where she met her future husband, Al. The severe "Depression" years limited the amount of salaries which they could earn but they lived happily on her teaching paycheck and his salary as a County Agricultural Agent in Cheboygan county.

During the WWII years they lived in Ionia, Michigan, mostly because this was a more productive food area. It was during these early years that their beloved son Roger and daughter Mary Ellen were born – thus increasing the family happiness two-fold! Both became distinguished special education teachers.

After the war Al served on the Staff at Michigan State University in the Cooperative Extension Service in East Lansing. Ellen continued to give piano lessons so that she could remain at home, but she also completed requirements for a master's degree in elementary education.

She now is reaping her rewards through music with her special friend T.G. Greenman, along with the residents at Independence Village, especially when they sing "How Great Thou Art" so beautifully.

From time to time a new resident has not been able to distinguish between Ellen and the author unless they are seen together but this has presented no problem.

Thelma Geraldine (T.G.) Greenman was born in North Dakota, raised and educated in Iowa, married a man from New York State, and lived there for forty years. Retirement took them to Mid-Florida and, following his death, she moved to Tucson, Arizona. Eventually her son, Philip, and his lovely wife enticed her to move nearer to her closely-knit family of two grandsons and wives, plus four great-grandchildren.

T.G. has often said that her life really began when she married her loving husband, Joseph, and they celebrated fifty years together. They traveled extensively throughout all fifty states and, since his death, she has visited England, Wales, New Zealand and the Fiji Islands.

Career-wise she did extensive office work which included the mastering of computers, was a personnel counselor, and assimilated a wealth of medical knowledge through her experiences as secretary to several physicians, and by following her son's medical training.

During her years of living in a retirement village in Florida, she served as musical director and played the organ for church services for ten years. She later sold her large Conn organ, disposed of a vast musical library and truly never expected to be actively involved in music again.

Very shortly after moving to Independence Village, she met Ellen Griffith who had already started a musical program for the residents. This was the beginning of a beautiful friendship as the two of them combined their special musical talents.

It has been a joy to watch these two work together! Each of them has definitely contributed the happiness of others.

While writing this particular chapter for my book about living at Independence Village, I am reminded of the very obvious changes during what I call "the changing of the guard" – both in management and in residents.

Whenever we find so many people living under the same roof we find a nucleus of many types of personalities and most of us are as contented as we make up our minds to be. As an author, this is all "grist for the mill" and I am indebted, especially, to those who have helped me understand the importance of knowing as many people as possible.

These two friends, Ellen and T.G., have helped me better understand behavior – both positive and negative – so that I can express myself even when under pressure. With Ellen I have always known that she will express her gratitude for my writing with a smile and a verbal "pat on the back." With T.G. I can always depend on her loyalty through reminders that I must say what I have to say without fear of adverse criticism. It was also she who alerted me to the need for getting information "straight from the horse's mouth whenever gossip or rumor became almost too much for me to handle.

31

I see in the friendship of these two very fine ladies a combination of organization power and the aesthetic skill which music has provided. As Aristotle once said, "Friendship is composed of a single sole inhabiting two bodies."

These folks will never forget the sweet sounds of yesteryear. ♥

The Reverend and His "Missus"

Shortly after arriving at her new home in Independence Village the author met two of the very finest people she had ever met as she was introduced to Dr. Paul Spierling and his lovely wife, Ruby. They were married on October 31, 1992, about one year following the death of his beloved wife, Marion, who was the sister of Ruby.

As the newlyweds were introduced in the pretty dining room, they were greeted by a loud and loving applause, accompanied by T.G. and Ellen who have been the backbone to most of our music and are loved and appreciated by all. The Monday night "Hymn Sings" and "Singalongs" have become a most welcome time for many. Later, when "Pinky" arrived on the scene with his donation of a *beautiful* organ to replace the smaller one, the music became even better.

Paul was born to German immigrant parents in north Milwaukee, Wisconsin, in 1899, where he attended public schools. He enlisted in the U.S. Army Medical Corps for eighteen months, twelve of them in France, and still has the special letter which he wrote to his parents on Armistice Day, November 11, 1918.

He served in ministries in many states while continuing his religious studies. In 1954 he became Associate Pastor at Broad Street Presbyterian Church in Columbus, Ohio, where he served for 20 years until his retirement in 1975.

While in Ohio he was granted a Doctor of Divinity degree and was very active in many phases of the Presbyterian Church U.S.A. while serving as a commissioner to the General Assemblies.

The marriage to Marion Johnson produced three children: Dr. Paul Spierling II, a gynecologist and obstetrician in New York; Reverend Ardith Hayes, Dean of Students in a Theological Seminary in

California; and Reverend M. Spierling, a Presbyterian minister in New Jersey. From these marriages Paul and Marion were blessed with eight grandchildren and five great-grandchildren.

One year after the death of Marion, Paul married her sister, Ruby, thus continuing a beautiful "family" relationship.

Ruby was born of Swedish immigrant parents on September 9, 1907, and was the seventh of eight children. She graduated from Lansing High School and still meets with her January class of these 67 years. Having received her BA and MA degrees from Michigan State University, she taught at Williamston High School, East Lansing High School, and finished her forty years as a teacher-counselor in Lansing, except for a one-year (1951-1952) period when she taught children of the U.S. Army in Nurenberg, Germany.

I needed only to talk with Ruby and Paul one or two times to realize what genuinely fine people they are! But the "frosting on the cake" came when I learned that she had taught with my beloved brother, Henry Noble.

"On the street (floor) where I live" I meet an excellent cross-index of the types of personalities which reside in Independence Village; the walkers who like this floor because of its convenient complete circle; the pool players; those who can walk on their own power; those who are, at times, confused; a few wheel chairs; and even a few in our laundry because of its convenient waiting area. It is here that I sometimes see Paul and Ruby because they can be together. Throughout a widowhood that spans more than 20 years I have learned to be far more than just a survivor, yet I sometimes envy those "hand holders" who cross my path. I am never *jealous* of them but sometimes wish that this could still happen for me. That is the basic difference between jealousy and envy. One is harmful and one is much more kind.

For several months I have been writing columns for newspapers and bulletins such as our own *Spotlight News* and it seems appropriate that I include one of these articles which depicts a very special relationship:

"Button Your Lip"

Often I have been guilty of wishing that people would be more careful about spreading news, no matter how innocent. Now it is I who must confess to *almost* starting a rumor here in Independence Village.

As I sat with friends consuming Root Beer floats I completely misunderstood a man when he said, "Did you know that Lupe (Guadalupes) hit a deer and nearly totaled her car?" Just at that moment our "Ruby" entered the room and I confess to telling the story to two or three persons, except that I said that *Ruby* had hit the deer!

Out of compassion I went directly to tell Ruby about my mistake and her reply to me will follow me for many days to come! Very quickly she said, "I didn't hit a deer. The only Dear I have is standing right here beside me and I haven't hit *him* – yet!"

You can imagine my chagrin as I ran the fast track to correct my story. What might never actually have ended up as malicious gossip simply scared me into the realization that even the most innocent remark could get out of hand!

The attitudes which so affect us in our "waning years" also influence the happiness of those around us and the quotes which this very special couple made when they were featured as "Resident of the Month" best depict how they continued to live their lives!

Paul – *"Independence Village is a wonderful place!"*

Ruby – *"Count your many blessings! Name them one by one!"*

May God continue to bless these two sweethearts, on earth as in Heaven.

A Hat is a Hat – For All That

"Vicki, Queen Mary and Di have all set the pace.
We followed like sheep, the whole female race.
Bea Lillie, bless her comedienne heart,
Had her own style, quite set apart.
Derbies and fezes, and Empress Eugenies –
A style in which, I promise, you will never see me!
Russian, Tyrolean, port-pie, sombrero –
Who would have thought the field was so narrow?
Fabulous jewels from Van Cleef and Arpels,
Perfume from Arden never repels.
But, 'hats' – be they pancakes, turbans or bee-hives,
It's Lily Dache's that made green-eyed the real wives.
Be-ribboned, be-spangles, fur-tailed or tasseled
In finding the right one we often were hassled.
But buy one we must, in time for the party
Where the style-setter turned up bare-headed, the smarty!
There are bonnets and tams, s'westerns and sailors,
Kepis and topees, burnosers and whalers.
Some are full-blossomed, some feathered and frilly.
Most all, you'll agree, are downrightfully silly.
For winter in Michigan – pass by haute couture.
Go simply bundled in woolen, to be really secure."

By Anita S. Frohnapfel, former resident of Independence Village
and special friend of the author.

From out of the blue someone mailed to me a complimentary ticket
to a special luncheon sponsored by the Detroit Area Writers Group
and the Detroit News. I may never know "from whence" this

invitation came but someone cared enough about me or about my writing skills to spend $17 on me. I'll settle for that.

Since I have long been enamored by the beauty of *hats* I decided to wear my very special new purple one. I had purchased it, on the spur of the moment, to wear with an outfit which I hope to wear at a book signing.

From the moment that I walked into the elegant Manor which housed this twelve hundred member audience, I faced an exciting challenge – and the hat was my refuge!

For the first few moments, as I wandered around the lobby, I was the *only* woman wearing a hat but, by the end of the program, I had spotted four (including my own) and I came up with four possible motivators for the wearing of the hats.

One woman was such a glaring example of "Haute Coutour," even with elbow-length gloves, that she would be recognized as a glamorous lady – even by those who might disapprove. As we visited, she talked of her recent mini-vacation at some plush resort where she took along six hats with matching gloves!

The woman who appeared to be accompanying her mumbled something about having wanted to wear a hat for the luncheon, but that she was afraid that it might obstruct the view of others. I made a mental note to add this tidbit to my repertoire of "the games that people play" and recorded it in my notebook as soon as I was out of sight.

A second hat obviously was attempting to cover an unkempt hairdo, with several limp and oily strands peeking out. She looked awful!

The third hat was so inconspicuous that my usually observant eye almost missed it. In other words, it did absolutely nothing for the trendy long-skirted outfit with which it was worn. Neither did it do anything to add to my very special day.

Then there was *mine* – which had been purchased at a fashion outlet mall on a whim as I modeled it and instantly met with approval of several bystanders. Two or three of them descended upon me to proclaim that the hat was "tre chic" but I paid little attention to them. Although I knew that the hat looked very stylish on me, I was also aware of a well-known sales pitch.

It was not until I looked in the mirror and saw my daughter-in-law making the "OK" signal with thumb and forefinger that I said to myself, *"This hat is for me!"*

On the drive home I reminisced about having moved to the city from a dream home in the country twenty years ago, at the time when I became a widow. I realized, belatedly, that I had left several hats in the closet of the country home but, perhaps because I was not seeing many hats being worn, I just never went back to retrieve them. Yet, for me, a pretty hat is never out of style and it does, somehow, add a touch of class.

In that closet I left a very glamorous chapeau made of feathers from a wild pheasant which had been shot in our back yard; an elegant wide-brimmed hat of black velvet, much like that I had seen on the head of a beautiful woman at the funeral of her husband. In fact, I had been the matron-of-honor for their wedding.

Yet another wide-brimmed hat made of straw had become so limp in such humid summer weather that I sprayed it with clear shellac. I remember holding the hat out the car window and, literally, praying that it would dry on the way to an important wedding.

Inside the church everything went very well but in the garden, where part of the ceremony was being held, the shellac began to melt – and *smell!* Actually, I remember tossing the hat into a dumpster while naming it my "sad hat."

Last, but not least, there was an adorable small turban of white fur (probably rabbit) which I called my "no slouch hat" because a much younger brother-in-law once used those words to describe me when I wore it to a basketball game in which he was a star.

On my return home from the Authors Luncheon I was reminded of a very special neighbor who had modeled for me the hat which she had worn as "bait" for the man she later married. We laughed about how, perhaps, it might work for *me* if I were to wear it publicly – even at retirement age.

Up until a few years ago I would have considered this possibility, but I am now "dedicatedly" married to my writing! ♥

A Music Box Love

"Lull'd in the countless chambers of the brain,
Our thoughts are link'd by many a hidden chain;
Awake but one, and lo, what myriads rise!
Each stamps its image as the other flies."
– Pope

Throughout most of our lives we have a tendency to "collect" and it is from these collectibles that we often glean our richest rewards of thinking.

Very shortly after the death of my beloved husband, Mac, my eyes became riveted on a beautiful life-size ceramic owl as I wandered restlessly throughout a special art studio. In fact, after returning several times to take another look, my companion for the day convinced me that I *must* purchase the object of my admiration. She had known of a special monetary gift from close friends where we managed a Pharmacy for more than twelve years and felt that I should use the money for something which would bring me a special happiness at this difficult time of my life.

However, I waited several days for the purchase, before realizing that, subconsciously, this owl appealed to me because of memories from my past.

Early in our marriage my husband was involved in a dreadful accident while playing softball in a community sponsored program for raising money. While literally being tackled when sliding into third base he suffered fractures and dislocations of the vertebrae at the base of the skull.

Details of this situation are of no purpose in this story except for the fact that is was necessary to shave his head and when the hair grew back it was *white!*

Actually, the new hair color was very striking because of his young face but, at times, he resented that his hair was not as brown as mine. On one such occasion I remember saying to him, "Well, anyway Honey, you are my wise old owl."

The collection of owl figurines and paintings grew to the extent that there came a time when I needed to call a halt. Even then, this urge for collecting continued to remain as a favorite hobby.

During one of my periods of reminiscing there came the memory that the only movie which we ever viewed more than once was "Dr. Zhivago." Both of us fell in love with the heroine, Lara, and with the song of the same title. Coincidentally, I became interested in music boxes – especially unusual ones.

Often as I browsed in specialty shops during the months that followed I found myself on the lookout for a special music box which played the theme song, "Farewell, My Love," from the Dr. Zhivago film. This was partially due to the fact that my husband had asked me to purchase such an item if I ever found it, along with his promise to pay me for it. Little did he know at the time that it was to become a "death wish."

After moving to the East Lansing area I soon became drawn to the lovely music box shops and it was here that, one day, I found my special "Lara" – and in a lovely ceramic *owl.*

It found its special place on a corner shelf of an "etagere" which holds many of my special mementos and it was here that it met with destruction from a windstorm, because of being too close to an open window. I remember that I wept because it was the only item on those shelves which I had hoped to retain for the rest of my life.

However, much to my amazement, only the musical element was destroyed, while the ceramic owl remained intact. It did, of course, send me searching for a replacement which I finally found in a beautiful heart-shaped wooden box with the hand-carved words, "I love you" on its lid. It repeatedly played only the first few words of "Lara" but it is a thing of beauty!

As I removed the lid from the box I soon realized that it was intended for small items of jewelry so I went searching for something special which would remind me, even more, of my love for Mac. To my surprise I discovered a charm bracelet which he had designed for me and would not let me see it until it was completely finished. It was not made of gold or silver, but it truly was "precious" to me because of the inventiveness of the person who designed it.

The charms were the size of a penny and cemented to them were miniature photos of my husband and son and daughter. There was also a tiny gold heart with the inscription, "If you need me, whistle!" I immediately recalled that this was the favorite term of endearment which Humphrey Bogart used to express his love for Lauren Bacall. There was also a miniature whistle at one time but it has disappeared.

I recall that there were moments when Mac was silent for so long a period of time as he retreated to his favorite den which housed his ham radio equipment that I called to ask him what he was doing. His reply was, "It's none of your business – and don't you dare come in here!"

As so often happens in my life (as with most writers) there has been an unusual repercussion to all this about owl and music boxes. While Christmas shopping in Chicago (1991) I turned to my daughter with an object in my hand and asked, "What does this key ring remind you of?" because on it was a two inch gold whistle.

Not another word was said but, on Christmas day, the very special key ring appeared along with my hoard of gifts. No one needed to tell me how it got there but that whistle may even have saved my life at one time when I was approached by an intruder while walking in the Mall. Another time it frightened away a small group of teenagers who were shooting pellets at the door of my parked car!

It is no wonder that my words of appreciation have never seemed quite adequate when I attempted to say, "Thank you" to the person (or persons) who returned this special key ring to the Merchants Service Center at the Frandor Mall in Lansing after finding it in the snow-covered parking lot. This happened on Valentine's day (1994) and I placed a note of appreciation in the Lansing State Journal within days. I probably shall never know whether it was read by those for whom it was intended but the whole incident has restored my faith in human nature – right at a time when it sometimes seems most important.

As I started to write this chapter for my book about living in Independence Village I immediately thought of how *much* our beloved Marketing Director, Lara Chandler, has enriched my life by "warming the cockles of my heart." I have told her about this and she now knows that my lovely music box which plays the tune bearing her name is to belong to her when I no longer need it. In fact, her name is on the bottom of the box and my family has been instructed to see that she gets it.

I am probably one of the few residents who pronounces her name as "Lara" and not "Laura." She does not mind having her name mispronounced, any more than I do mine, but to me she has the same glowing beauty as that of "Lara" in my favorite movie and book, "Dr. Zhivago."

It is with great pride that I dedicate this chapter to her! ♥

Courage from a Wheelchair

"The truly brave are soft of eyes and heart,
And feel for what their duty bids them do."
– Byron

One does not need to go far in order to find another person who is stronger than himself, if he will but look into the eyes of a person who is confined to a wheelchair or walker. At no time in my life has this been more evident than when living in an independent retirement community.

I continue to be one of the fortunate few who has found an even greater compassion than I realized was mine as I talk with several of these people who do not consider themselves as "handicapped."

Recently, I talked with Marsden Wilson, who was living at Independence Village and it was this communication that sent me to the word processor for the writing and editing of this chapter. I had to do so immediately because the "notes" which I had gathered were in my head, rather than in a notebook which I usually carry with me.

For several months I had suspected that Marsden might, at one time, have been a teacher. It has become almost instinctive for me to sort these people out and much of the time I am right.

Humorously, I must confess that this type of judgement might be related to the fact that my beloved Mac often told me that he could "spot a school teacher a mile away" and, occasionally, I felt that his inference was *not* too complimentary. On one occasion, when listening to this type of remark, I even bristled – to the extent that I said to him, "Tell me six characteristics of a teacher" as you see that person.

The result was that we *both* ended up in hilarious laughter when we realized that not *one* of these traits fit *me*. And, here I was, the teacher whom he had known the most and the longest.

As I visited with Marsden we discovered that, except for a differential of ten years, we might have crossed paths many years ago. As an educator, he had taught many children and had served as an administrator in several schools which were within my area of reference. Some of our students from Michigan State University had served as student teachers in schools where he had served as the Principal. Although they were not within my jurisdiction, they might have been had I arrived on the scene ten years earlier.

I had observed this man as he progressed from a basic type of walker to what he called his "Cadillac" because of all the conveniences attached to his electric wheelchair. I never once heard him complain, although I know from the expression in his eyes that he was in great pain. Learning that he had suffered from MS (Multiple Sclerosis) for more than thirty years and still felt that life was worth living made me want to scream at some of the people who have so much less to complain about.

I learned that Marsden had two great loves – his family and his summer home in northern Michigan. In fact, his plans were to go to this home for the summer months, although I had a gut feeling that this would not happen for him in 1993.

I had seen him with several of his grandchildren who adored him and let him know that they did. I remember his description of how excited he often felt as nineteen members of his family gathered for special days in their homes. One of them I remember in particular for she is actively involved with seminars which help older people retain their feeling of self-esteem. I remember thinking, "This girl is a *natural.*"

The uncanny part of this story is that I took this article with me to read to my entire family at Easter and, on my return, learned that this kind man was in the hospital for his final visit. In fact, he passed away the following day.

I wish now that I had taken the time to say, "Thank you" for the inspiration he had given me. Perhaps, I can compensate by getting in touch with another friend many miles away – if only to remind her that I love her. She has suffered with this same vicious disease for many years, yet has been a prolific artist. Her paintings have been on exhibit and even surgery of *both* hands did not halt her.

She will be so happy to hear from me. ♥

Par for the Course

It is such great *fun* to write my story about Cecil and Evelyn McKay because I have known them since 1981 when I moved across the hall from them in the Pine Forest apartment complex (known now as Hidden Tree). Actually, I knew Evelyn a few months prior to that when I was on a tour to Mackinaw Island and she was our tour guide.

She overheard me say that I was looking for an apartment and was very quick to inform me that there would be one available in her building but she did not tell me that it was, at that time, occupied by Cecil while they made the necessary plans for him to move across the hall.

I remember that the apartment was so well furnished that I purchased the carpeting and drapes from Cecil, mostly because they were probably better than I could have afforded to buy. He had impeccable taste in such matters and still has. In fact, since coming to Independence Village, I remember telling him on New Year's Eve that "If he lives to be 100 he will still be a fashion plate!" For this compliment I received one of his ingratiating smiles.

Cecil grew up in Croswell, Michigan, and attended Central High School and Ferris College (now Ferris State University). Evelyn grew up in Minneapolis, Minnesota, where she went to South High School. Later she attended the University of Minnesota.

Cecil married Evelyn Anderson Bauer in 1980 and they resided across the hall from me for over eight years. We were good neighbors who respected each other's privacy while, also, enjoying good conversation from time to time. Prior to this marriage Cecil had three children and Evelyn two.

It was interesting to watch the growing devotion of this fine couple while Cecil continued to be active with his business and producing the most beautiful flower gardens and Evelyn served as Social Director for the apartment complex.

At that complex there was a lovely walk-through courtyard and people often took that route because of Cecil's gorgeous flowers. We still kid each other about the fact that *my* flowers would never have survived without Cecil's frequent TLC.

In this courtyard there was a tree stump in which a ninety year-old man had carved an old man seated. Many people abhorred this carving, even to the extent of claiming that it looked like an old man going to the toilet – but to *me* it was *beautiful* because it represented the efforts of an old man who still took tremendous pride in his ability to produce sculpture. In fact, I was so intrigued by this piece of art that I searched and found a formula for preserving it against weather damage. An occasional observer remarked that its destruction would be a blessing. Another "kind soul" admitted that she could understand my appreciation IF I were a connoisseur of Picasso paintings.

At that time, of course, I wasn't, but I certainly began to study them and even purchased a large handbag made from fabric which was stamped with some of his art figures. How I wish I had that handbag in my possession today.

The McKays owned the McKay Coal Company, McKay Lumber Company and McKay Golf and Country Club properties in the Lansing area. While in Minnesota, Evelyn was office manager for Egequist Bakery and, later, she worked at Bauer Pastry Shop in Lansing.

Both Cecil and Evelyn remain very active in the community and here at Independence Village. Cecil attends Central Methodist Church and Evelyn is a member of St. Thomas Aquinas Catholic Church.

In high school Cecil was a member of the orchestra and later played in Masonic Marching bands in several parades in Chicago and Cincinnati. He belonged to the Elks and Masons.

In addition to Evelyn's various duties as a social director, she was President of the Catholic Women's Club, Treasurer of the East Lansing Women's Club and started a Widow's Club. While living at Pine Forest she helped start a Neighborhood Watch with the East Lansing Police Department, while also serving as a tour director for the East Lansing Older Peoples' Program.

How well I remember the harrowing New Year's weekend experience which this couple had in a hotel in Chicago, Illinois. They had made reservations for a fun-filled occasion which included an all-night dance in the ballroom but, while riding the elevator, a "pick-pocket" relieved Cecil of his billfold! In fact, the thief was so clever that Cecil did not even miss the wallet until reaching for it in his hip pocket.

The wallet contained a substantial amount of cash which was never regained but the most serious ramification was when they returned to their Pine Forest apartment and discovered that Evelyn's automobile was missing from the carport. It had never occurred to them that carrying an extra key to her car in his billfold would create a hazard. Apparently there was identification which led to the carport location.

The theft was immediately reported to the police department and, several days later, the car was found in a warehouse parking lot in Lansing – none the worse for wear.

About two weeks later the billfold was hand delivered by a messenger. It contained several credit cards and identification but, of course, no *cash*. Because there may have also been a key to their apartment in the billfold, I remember that the door locks had to be changed. It proved to be a valuable lesson to many of us but, most of all, we were glad that our special couple had received no bodily harm.

At Independence Village both Cecil and Evelyn are involved in many activities. Cecil keeps our courtyard beautiful with flowers, bird feeders and birdbaths which provide pleasures for everyone to behold. Evelyn is our librarian and serves on the Activities committee where she contributes many hours of service.

Close observance of Cecil and Evelyn McKay reminds us that "Our happiness in this world depends on the affections we are enabled to inspire." (Duchesse de Preslin.)

A Family Love Affair

Not many months following my arrival in Independence Village I met Marshall Simpson as he returned to East Lansing to take residence here, prior to the arrival of his wife, Blanche.

Marshall is a very intense man and whenever he makes his appearance people *look* and *listen.* I, personally, was amazed at how quickly he had assessed the situation and how capably he was paving the way for the arrival of his wife who had remained, temporarily, with a daughter in California.

It did not take long for me to realize that an entire family was settling into a new living situation, especially after meeting the exuberant daughter, Barbara, from nearby Okemos. Without her loyalty and devotion I might not have been quite as aware of what was going on. At one time when I said to her, "Barbara, I simply do not know how you *do* all that you do for and with your parents," she replied, "They took good care of me all of my formative years with a great deal of self-sacrifice. Now it is *my* turn to return the favor."

I also think that one of the reasons that Barbara intrigues me most is that I see my own daughter, Judie, as I watch her in action. Perhaps it is their intense love of children through their teaching that makes them persons of deep compassion. Perhaps it is because I, too, am a teacher.

Marshall Simpson was born in Lacota, Michigan on August 22, 1912, and attended grade school there for eight years. His father was a hardware merchant in Lacota for fifty years, having graduated from Kalamazoo College. His mother graduated from Eastern Michigan University and both parents were teachers in their early years. She, in fact, was Marshall's teacher in grades 6-8. It has reminded me of how both my son and daughter were my pupils in grade 4 in Nashville, Michigan. It was one of those experiences which I would not take a million dollars for but would never want to repeat! I learned *much* from my children. I'm not too sure how much they learned from me.

Marshall graduated from South Haven High School in 1929 and graduated with an AB degree from Western Michigan State College (now WMU) in 1933.

He taught in Constantine, Michigan for one year; Owosso High School for ten years; Eastern High School in Lansing, Michigan for thirty years. In Owosso he was athletic manager and secretary of the Saginaw Valley Athletic Association.

Marshall enjoyed many accomplishments through his membership in several social and professional organizations. Among these were life memberships in the Michigan and National Teacher Associations, the Michigan Retired Teacher's Association and the Masonic Lodge. He is a past president of the Old News Boys of Greater Lansing and the Audubon Club at local, state and national levels.

For over twenty years he served as an Athletic official, both at high school and college levels, which perhaps accounts for his avid interest in sports even in retirement.

He and Blanche moved to Florida in 1975 where he escorted tours around the world; eighteen cruises; six times to Hawaii; three times to Alaska; New Zealand twice; Fiji Islands twice; the Pacific Rim; South America twice; the Amazon, Nile and Orinico rivers; and countries which included Egypt, Greece, Spain, Portugal, Morocco, Kenya, Rodesia and Africa.

Closer to home he made three round-trips across Canada; the Rose Bowl and the Orange Bowl several times.

Blanche and Marshall have three daughters who, like their mother, graduated from Michigan State University. From these marriages they now have nine grandchildren and two great-grandsons. One of these great-grandsons is sometimes seen with a big, happy grin as he rides on grandpa's electric wheelchair throughout the halls of our village.

It is this very special wheelchair that intrigues me as I watch Marshall manipulate it with great skill – and speed, whenever possible.

The Marshall Simpson automobile is parked just below my window so that I have ample opportunity to observe the tremendous skill and patience it takes for Marshall to maneuver himself into the driver's seat. Occasionally, I have even felt pangs of guilt as I watch this transaction – partly because I have never heard any grumbles or groans from the driver.

It is most essential that he continue to have times when he simply can "get away from it all" – just as it is for most of us.

On the two or three times when I have had the chance to converse with Blanche I have learned that we have so much in common because of our concerns that children need, above all else, to be able to communicate. Which, of course, includes *reading.*

Because of our common interest in teaching reading methods to children and adults we sometimes had a moment or two of understanding as we simply nodded our heads in agreement. It is only natural that the daughter, Barbara, would also be able to communicate with me because of her continuous efforts to catch pre-school children with her enthusiastic approach.

In addition to this common thread which is woven into the lives of the two of us, I have learned that Barbara attended high school with my nephew, Charles Noble, who is the son of my beloved brother, Henry Noble. In fact, he has informed me that he actually had a "crush" on her at one time and that, now that he has seen her as a lovely, mature woman he probably should have pursued that further!

Soon after learning that Marshall and Blanche had transferred their membership in the Teacher's Credit Union in Owosso to the Lansing Teacher's Credit Union in Lansing in 1945, I realized that Marshall was Vice-President for several of the years that Henry was Treasurer/ Manager. It is, indeed, a small, small world.

Occasionally, for a change of pace, I read my morning paper while sitting in the beautiful lobby of our Village and it is here that Marshall and I sometimes discuss important (and unimportant) topics of interest. He also borrows my paper just long enough to study the Bridge hand for the day. At first he did this spontaneously, without my being on the scene, until he had a chance to say to me, "I was sure that you wouldn't mind."

I sometimes chuckle as I realize that Marshall has gotten to my paper first, simply because of the way in which he returns that section to its counterparts.

It adds a touch of humor to my day!

What Price Succotash?

Although I am very pleased with the cuisine at Independence Village most of the time, it is good to "eat out" occasionally. When I do so, it is usually at a favorite family type restaurant where I have made a habit of taking along my note pad and pen because it is here that I often find human interest stories that keep me in touch with what some people call "the outside world."

As I studied the menu of one of my favorite restaurants and debated over the choice of two vegetables, my mind flashed back nearly sixty years!

Childhood memories "reared their happy heads" to remind me of a mother who sometimes held her brood together with her ability to control an entire family through her culinary skills. Never have I found even *one* cook who could surpass her in concocting a menu of astonishing variety, for a family of seven, on a weekly budget of $17.50.

Now that I think about it, that allowance never changed over a period of twenty years. The food on that table was as delectable in 1940 as it was in 1920.

I swear that, today, this woman could prepare a meal which would serve ten people – just from the left-overs that accumulate in my refrigerator over a period of two or three weeks.

Whenever prices soared, we simply adjusted by growing more of our own vegetables or accepting donations from farmers as medical payment to my physician father. In fact, he established what may have been the first hot lunch program in Michigan schools in the 1920s by using food donations, especially staples, from these same farmers.

I remember that my mother showed no favoritism as she doled out specific chores for her children. We took turns at desprouting potatoes in the dark, dank basement where we hoped to never come eyeball to eyeball with *mice.*

Somehow, there seemed to be no end to that pile of potato eyes that stared out in the dark!

I remember being a part of the whole process in the preparation of my mother's favorite *succotash* at the early age of eight. There was always the husking of the donated sweet corn and the shelling of the lima beans which we grew on our own two acres right in the middle of the village.

Everything had to be "same day fresh" and the cooking began with cold water which was supposed to bring out the natural flavor. It is interesting that today we still feel this way about brewing good coffee.

When tender, the corn and the lima beans were drained and the water was replaced by milk (or cream), butter, salt and pepper until it became a succulent delicacy.

Recently, I prepared this concoction to serve to cousins who had almost forgotten what a special treat it was. It was too early in the season for freshly grown corn and lima beans. The best I could do was to use frozen vegetables and, somehow, it was not quite the same – but it was still *good.*

As I sat in the restaurant I suddenly realized that I would need to create my own succotash from the menu by ordering a dish of corn and a dish of lima beans as a side order. Somehow, this is a delicacy which I create best in my own kitchen – but never with vegetables that have been canned.

I remember, also, raising a crop of asparagus in our back yard and how it seemed to be my responsibility to cut it, wash it and bundle it in 1# bunches. Probably this was because my father taught me one of the first lessons in economics by purchasing for me a little red wagon from which I delivered and sold the asparagus at a price of $.15 per bunch.

The plan was for me to earn enough to repay my father one-half the amount of the cost of the red wagon.

A few years later I advanced to a higher level of finance as my father loaned me the money to purchase *one gross* of a gadget called

"Clever Claws" which was intended for removing obstacles from difficult places – such as narrow-mouthed bottles.

It became a door-to-door sales attempt which I readily learned to abhor! To this day I am so uncomfortable about selling tickets (even for a worthy cause) for charity that I inevitably end up purchasing the entire batch.

The greatest legacy that I have learned and earned from this entire process is that, whenever possible, one must finish what one starts to do. It carries over into my enthusiasm for my retirement freelance writing, while I see people all around me who have simply lost the zest for living. Occasionally, someone tells me that my positive attitude has rubbed off on others. Several have told me that this particular story about succotash and asparagus has stirred similar memories for them.

This is enough for me!

From the Other Side of the Room

Recently, I decided to move from the table in the dining room where I sat for several months in order to meet other residents who remained as strangers to me. It is important that an author move around frequently in order to get new stories. It had even occurred to me that, perhaps, I "had stayed too long at the Fair," although this was a self-imposed decision.

It has been interesting to note that, no matter where I sit, there will always be interesting people to provide me with new ideas for the book which I am writing about living in Independence Village.

Just as I shall continue to find sadness, I shall also find a terrific amount of gladness; just as I shall continue to find grumpiness, I shall continue to find humor! That is what life is all about and it seems to keep all of us hanging on with all our might.

On one side of the room I sat so near to the kitchen that I could see the notice on the wall which indicated B for Back and F for Front. Although I felt certain that the signs were intended for kitchen and serving staff it amused me that, occasionally, a resident became indignant whenever the serving was started at the wrong end of the dining room. Upon investigation it was learned that, sometimes, even the wait persons were confused. However, it must be remembered that it is no easy task to serve 160 people and please them most of the time!

It has never bothered me whether I was served first or last or whether I was served coffee early or late, but I *do* respect the rights of others to make these decisions. For many, the dinner hour is the most important time of day and these people are certainly evidence of the need for "living to eat."

Although I have long been a proponent of the need for congeniality which visiting at the dining table can provide, I have always been so busy that "eating to live" has become my motto. Never has there been a time when I could not make a meal out of what the menu provides by simply eating more of the foods that I like and ignoring that which does not tempt my palate. For some people this is a difficult decision. I recognize that. Since "open seating" has been declared, I am finding a great deal of pleasure in moving about from table to table. Apparently, there are just as many fine people on one side of the room as on the other – and just as many heads of white hair!

It has reminded me of my beloved Anita who formerly lived here and who was partially responsible for influencing me to move here. Never has she failed to help me see the funny side of a situation where I have been tempted to be even the least bit discouraged by an unkind remark deliberately intended to hurt. Rather than saying the customary, "Consider the source," she has always made me laugh.

At one time, when I was especially upset because someone had spoken an unkind word of me, she said, as she hugged me, "Just think, my dear, of that large sea of white-haired old ladies and remember that *you* have been given a very distinct title which none of the others can claim!"

Sad as the situation was, she made me happier as I accepted the fact that this sort of thing is always going to happen. I have inherited a beautiful sense of humor from my mother and it has seen me through many difficult situations.

I have been writing an on-going chapter of humorous events while living here at Independence Village but there is one, which has happened since my decision to become a "floater" in the dining room, that I want to tell now. Although I feel certain that the person involved would not mind my mentioning her name, I prefer just to relate the conversation. To her I said, "Your hair looks *beautiful* today. Do you have it done every week?" Her reply was, "I've never worn a *wig* in my entire life!" The longer I live, the more I realize how many people have hearing difficulties, just as many of them must think that I mumble.

Harry Harris, one of our more elderly residents, has granted me permission to include in my book one of his cleverly written discussions which would help all of us have more compassion for the hard of hearing. I thank him for this.

From another male resident I received the example of an anecdote that comes "close" to being suggestive, yet manages to remain what some people would label as "clean." Since it appeared in Reader's Digest, we decided that it was perfect for my book.

At a nudist camp where several senior citizens were residing, one gentleman had grown a beard which touched the ground. When another asked of him, "Why did you let your beard grow to such lengths for a nudist camp?" Without cracking a smile, his response was, "Somebody's gotta' go for coffee!"

Most of the time I am concerned that I simply do not think of the right answer to a question asked of me by a fellow resident. Occasionally, I *do* come up with a good one – such as when someone asked me whether I had become accustomed to the "organized slop" served by the kitchen and I responded, "I haven't had any." Later, when telling this to a visitor (one of my former college students) he said, "You could have said that you guess you missed that meal."

When I first arrived at the Village there was an appeal for "two seatings" in the dining room and, eventually, this came about. It was not long before some of the residents who wanted this arrangement most became the instigators for a change back to *one* seating. I feel certain that there was justification for this reasoning which new management seemed ready to accept.

Almost immediately there was an outcry when designated name tags were removed from the tables. Personally, I was in agreement with the decision because I had visited a prison and a mental institution where this had been a requirement simply out of necessity. However, it continues to make no difference to me whether I am labeled or not at the dining table. I continue to feel that it *never* will be possible to please all of the people all of the time and I would not like the task of even trying to do so!

I am *happy* to report that I continue to find that 95% of the residents at Independence Village are as contented as they have made up their minds to be. This is whether they sit on the same side of the room with me – or even down the middle. ♥

Tony Award

Prior to moving to Independence Village I resided at Raleigh House Apartments where I met Anita Frohnapfel and where a very special friendship had its birth.

Having transferred from a very sad three month rental situation, following more than nine years of happiness there, I sometimes needed to pinch myself in order to believe that I had found such a beautiful spot!

I am an extremely independent and self-sufficient person who shall be forever grateful to the people who welcomed me at the Raleigh House complex with open arms, especially since launching my retirement freelance writing.

Much of my summer writing during my two-year stance was done from a comfortable chair on my patio which overlooked a small wooded area where my bird feeder lured many friendly wings and where I sometimes saw deer in winter.

Friendly neighbors, along with a very capable apartment manager, extended so many kindnesses that I needed to accept them with gratitude while not allowing them to be overly protective of me.

Many of my human interest stories are gleaned while sitting in the malls and restaurants where I can observe people from all walks of life, yet it was in my miniature garden of paradise that I often put the final touches with my ever-ready pen and paper. Like the Energizer battery, the pen "goes on and on."

My very first experience as I browsed for a new apartment was enhanced by the acceptance from one of the most charming ladies I ever expect to meet. In fact, as I was introduced to her, she invited me in and, literally, gave me a sales talk about the advantages of living there. I do not often make such decisions impulsively but, this time, I did and it was "Miriam" who tipped the scales for me.

Almost before I could make connections with the manager I had made my decision. "Miriam" had told him about my visit and had urged him not to let this one slip through his fingers.

There were people of all ages there, in an area which was originally intended for retirees, but there simply were not enough who either wanted or could afford to take up residence there.

I was so glad that it had worked out for me for I have always needed people of all ages around me.

Just beyond me there was a very nice retirement home and I told my family that when, or if, I could no longer live alone they might need only to go "over the hill and through the woods to grandmother's house." I have always known when the time had come for me to move on.

The summer before moving to Raleigh House my new friend, "Miriam", was critically ill and had purchased an adorable puppy whom she named "Tony." At that time I felt that he was the cutest dog I had ever seen, with his bull dog face and with head and paws stark white in color. I was told that the black which is usually around the eyes of this breed was on the stomach of Tony as black polka dots on white. Such unusual coloring occurs very rarely in Boston Bull Terriers. I had found an unusual dog and an unusual lady!

As Tony learned that he could control the habits of his mistress he, literally, saved her life by tugging at her blanket and demanding that she get out of bed and take him for periodic walks. Most of us who came to love him realized that he had become very protective of his mistress. For this he deserved the "Tony Award" – but so did she!

As I concluded this miniature dissertation I said another "Thank You, God" for having steered me in the right direction. I was reminded of another friend who once asked me why I talk to God so often. When telling this to one of my favorite ministers (Carl Staser) and saying that my answer was, "Because *He* is my friend," the minister replied, "That's very good. You could also have said that *He* is the only one who really listens."

I informed Tony's mistress that I usually do not reveal the actual names of my "victims" in writing and her reply was that she really did not mind the use of her name but that she had always loved the name of "Miriam."

As I finally came to the conclusion of this tale I learned that "Miriam" had made the decision to move to Independence Village while still completely mobile, even though that meant giving up Tony. He would, however, live in a happy situation with his brother, Bud.

I knew that "Miriam" would adjust very well in her new retirement complex because she is such a gracious human being who will always acquire new friends all around her. To many she is the perfect example of "To have a friend you have to *be* one."

As her friend I know that I would never desert her simply because she moved away from my neighborhood. We both possess such similar qualities as compassion; the joy of living; and a built-in sense of humor which will "stand us in good stead."

I even thought it quite possible that she would pave the way for *me* when it comes time to move to a more protective living situation, with less physical responsibilities – but not until I realized that I actually "had my show on the road" with my retirement writing.

The One That Got Away

(A sequel to TONY AWARD, written by "Miriam.")

No, this is *not* a fish story! This is the story of Miriam who, for a totally unexplained reason, decided the time had come for her to live in the protective atmosphere of a retirement home.

She gave away furniture, china and silver. She gave away mementos of family and friends. She gave away bric-a-brac and a pair of porcelain candelabra dating back to 1840. But hardest of all, she gave away Tony, dating to June of 1990. He was a white-faced, unlovely Boston Terrier who would never make it in the show ring. She had raised Tony through the tedious puppy stages and had him as her darling for less than two years.

Miriam was the life of the party in her new surroundings. She walked with a spring in her step and her laugh was contagious as she soon learned the names of most of the residents at Independence Village. She enjoyed a friendship of a mildly amorous nature for a while. But, while as suddenly as she had chosen to live in these "Halls of I.V." so swiftly did she decide that this life was no longer interesting and she longed for unrestricted independence. And, of course, another Tony.

Miriam has been away from Independence Village for more than a year but she still values the friendships formed here and brings hugs and kisses all around whenever she visits. Life is good for her in her new home, with a new Boston Terrier now past his first birthday. "This Tony," she tells us, "of all the B.T.'s in my life is the prize of the catch!"

Tribute to a Gentle Woman

"Sweet speaking oft a currish heart reclaims."

– Sidney

As I searched my several references for a quotation which would best describe a lovely lady who I met and became acquainted with in Independence Village, I was delighted to also add a new word (currish) to my writing vocabulary.

From the very first time that I watched Mildred Quinn walking into our beautiful dining room until the final day that I saw her leave the building which I have learned to call "Home", I felt my life enriched by just walking beside her and listening to her soft words of wisdom.

This time I had the common sense to get to know someone before I decided that she *must* become a chapter in the book which I am writing about living in an independent retirement village.

On several occasions I have needed to write a chapter for this book without ever having had the opportunity to interview some of my favorite people. However, at such times, I have been lucky because a remaining spouse has been around to verify what I write.

Because I am meeting so many wonderful people, there never will be time enough to reach them all with my writing. It has become a *big* challenge to me.

Mildred Quinn had been a resident of East Lansing and prior to her retirement she had raised her family in the Detroit area. She passed away on July 21, 1993, and was predeceased by her husband, Arvie.

Surviving are four children: Arvie, Andrew, Adrian and Anita. It is interesting that she has bestowed "all A" names on her children.

She began her work career at OTAC and retired after a quarter of a century of auditing and supervising audits of tax returns at the

United States Internal Revenue Service. She was born in Memphis, Tennessee, attended Booker T. Washington High School, and attended West Virginia State University.

She loved family, shopping, and Bridge – perhaps in that order. How I wish I had known that she was a bridge player!

I can close my eyes today and see her as she graced the lobby which led to our lovely dining room. It was here that she sat for frequent conversation which has enriched my life and the many others who grew to love her.

I recall that she walked with a cane and that she carried one arm rigidly (sometimes in a sling) as the result of a stroke, but nothing destroyed her optimism. Although I walked beside her many times, and have asked the other ladies at her table, none of us could even remember which arm was incapacitated. It has even brought a smile to my lips as I realize how insignificant such information really is. It is what is commonly called a "petty detail."

I believe that I met all of her children and I recall wondering, many times, how such a petite woman had children who grew to be so *tall*. With a chuckle, it reminded me that I can easily walk under the arm of my son or two grandsons.

On one occasion I walked up to a fine looking young man and said, "You must be one of the handsome sons of Mildred Quinn!" His unexpected reply was, "Well, I happen to be a nephew, but I'll accept the compliment." For once, I did not become the victim of "foot in mouth disease" because my remark fit, in spite of the fact that it was not a son to whom I spoke.

On another occasion I remember carrying on a rather loud conversation with a friend (who was deaf) because we were so annoyed by malicious gossip. Out of the corner of my eye I noticed Mildred watching us. As I turned in her direction she said, "I want to hear kinder tones and see the return of the happy smiles to the faces of two people who have endeared themselves to many of us." *No one,* in my entire life, has ever done such a super job of "putting me in my place" without one ounce of resentment on my part!

From the day that I first met this lovely lady, until the last day that I encountered her in the lobby and realized how very sick she was, my life has been richer. I shall never forget her, for:

> "Grace was in all her steps, heaven in her eye,
> In every gesture, dignity and love."
> – *Milton* ♥

Band of Gold

Just a few months before moving to Independence Village I had started some research (definitely not scientific) about men wearing their wedding ring following death of a spouse. It became so interesting that I decided to continue it.

As I sat across the bridge table from a very fine gentleman, I was immediately intrigued by his wedding ring and a fond idea gave birth!

Because I knew that this man had recently become a widower, it started for me a chain reaction as to why people do, or do not, continue to wear that very special "band of gold."

While contemplating this particular situation and listening to his brief description of his wife's lingering illness and subsequent death, my thoughts turned inward.

First, I made a mental note that probably this man was advertising the fact that his was a happy marriage. Or, he might have been wearing the ring as a warning signal without realizing that he was doing so.

Because I recently "got too close to the fire" in a romantic situation, I have been on guard when I meet attractive men. I admit that it is refreshing to meet one of the opposite sex who is not using his very obvious charm to seduce women. By being thoughtful to *any* woman standing nearby, this new friend showed no partiality.

If she is putting on her coat, he assists her. If she is taking it off, he hangs it up. If she needs a more comfortable chair, he gets it for her. How refreshing!

As I speak of the "opposite sex" I am reminded of an adorable little boy in my classroom who said to a little girl, "Are you the opposite sex or am I?"

When my bridge partner said to me, "Are you advertising?" I jerked my thoughts to realize that he was talking about the card which I had played and I smiled as I realized that, quite accidently, I had discovered another human interest story worthy of my book.

Another friend, who had also lost his wife, continues to wear his wedding ring. I had not given it too much thought until now, but his decision may have been for yet another reason.

We had been family friends of fifty years so I knew that for many of those earlier years he had not worn a wedding ring. His grief has been difficult to watch and I may never get the chance to be a listening ear to him. As I've said to our mutual friends, "Bruce" and I are like siblings and have even changed diapers for each other's children, yet I probably will never again enter his home which I frequented for so many years." It leaves me a little sad yet there is no way that I would ever embarrass him – partly because I also loved his wife as I would a sister.

My nephew, who has been married twice, informs me that he sometimes finds himself feeling to see if his wedding ring is still on his finger. Facetiously, I have found myself wondering which ring he is referring to.

When my husband, Mac, passed away I made an emotional decision not to remove his wedding band. My rationalization at the time was that we could not afford two rings at the time of our wedding. I had also taken some kidding about purchasing the ring twenty years late.

The history of my own "band of gold" is stranger yet, for the first one had to be exchanged for white gold when my finger became allergic. In fact, we joked about whether I should "go platinum" should it become necessary.

This first ring was later melted into a gold nugget given to me by my daughter and her husband after discovering it in the drawer of a table which I had given them. It is now resting in a bank security box because a thief tried in vain to snatch it from my neck.

Strangely enough, I now wear a wedding band which encompasses two diamonds – my own and that of my beloved sister. Because she never married, she wore the diamond which our mother had worn.

I wear this wedding band on my right hand because of arthritis. It is the hand which taught me to accept arthritis both with respect and with humor.

Once, when I pointed from the window of our beautiful country home, my husband asked, "Which direction are you pointing?" Because he was a very kind man I instinctively knew that he was helping me accept an infirmity which will never stop my writing career. I can always dictate my stories to a tape recorder and I have discovered that, if necessary, I could "talk" to a computer.

On my left hand I sometimes wear a very special custom-designed silver ring which I inherited from my brother. At the time of his death I was so heart-broken that I relinquished his ring to a dresser drawer. Six years later, at the wedding of his son, I realized that it was time to get the ring out of its hiding place. I affectionately call it my "badge of honor" as I feel nothing but compassion and love following a few years of turmoil. During my lifetime many sad situations have also provided me with a chuckle or two and this was no exception.

The man who was, originally, the inspiration for this story, has now moved on and many of us will miss him. He did, however, return to town a few times and on one occasion I talked with him. I also noticed that he was *not* wearing the special "band of gold."

Characters I Have Met and More

This is a slightly revised title which was suggested by John Smith, one of our more affable residents, after listening to me relate some of the humorous incidents which I have been encountering.

John is a thoroughbred Scotsman, having been born in Scotland and continuing to use the "Scottish Brogue" even after living in the United States more than thirty-five years. To me it is delightful but I often have to interpret what he says for other people. Sometimes the interpretation is hilarious because of a complete change of meaning.

At one time I attempted to write the "Biography of John Smith" but had to discard the idea when the dialect did not come through distinctly on my tape recorder. I also did not do my best interviewing, perhaps because John was uncomfortable when responses did not come easily for him. It was by mutual consent that we discontinued the interview.

We did, however, send one tape to John's sister who still lives in Scotland and she was overjoyed. Hearing his voice whenever she wants must be a real pleasure for her, although John does talk with her by phone every month.

John Smith will always be remembered for his sense of humor, his friendliness and for having a genuine interest in helping others. He has helped me want to put into written words some of the almost weird experiences from the dining room, the lobby and the hallways. Most of them have added a touch of humor to the routine living in a community retirement village.

During the moving-in weekend when my family helped me arrange and rearrange my furniture and many belongings, we discovered that the leaking toilet which I had reported with a work order had now become an emergency situation. This presented my first serious problem, for Harold, our maintenance man, is not available on weekends.

By the end of the day my helpers had convinced me that I could "get by" with turning the water off and on so that I could use the toilet until it could be repaired on Monday.

However, when I was forced to hurry to the restroom near the elevator, I felt little comfort in the advice that the walking would be good for me! It also occurred to me that I should not be walking in the halls in my house robe – until the thought came to me that anyone who might see me there at 2:00 A.M. probably should not be there either.

The maintenance man showed up at my door at 10:30 on Monday morning, shortly after I had phoned the desk that I was getting concerned about the residents who might be living below me. I now had every bath towel I could get my hands on, plus a large braided rug, snuggled around the base of the toilet.

I must admit that Harold certainly knows his job. I just hope that my future emergencies happen while he is on the premises.

I ended up giving him one of my favorite wall plaques because I had no spot for it. The slogan was *Love One Another* and, for a brief moment when he hesitated, I thought I might be forced to remind him that is was a message directly from the Bible.

A few days later I met the assistant manager driving into the parking area just as I was leaving it. As he asked, "Is everything all right?" I informed him that I had needed to return to the desk for keys and hoped that I would also find my *head*. Little did I know, at that time, that one of the most prevalent petty problems which residents contribute is the loss of their keys. So much humor has been evident in the dining room that I often carry a notebook in order to keep track of the better ones. My initiation to this was when a resident came on the run toward me as I stood by the fireplace in the dining lobby. As she yelled, "Out of my way, everybody. I gotta' go and when you gotta' go – you gotta' go!" I looked around me and did not see another person within fifty feet, but she gave me a shove which, fortunately, landed me on the davenport.

I was once seated at a table where a resident often came up with a witty remark even when discouraged by delayed service. One day we had waited an unusually long period of time and she said, "Have we eaten yet?" She honestly could not remember whether we might have been served.

From that same table one of the residents returned from the salad bar and soon discovered a gold filling from a tooth on her plate. The rest of us were stunned over the possibilities of how this had happened, until she realized that the filling was from her *own* mouth.

At that same salad bar I was walking behind a gentleman when he turned to me in panic as his hearing aid fell into the greens which surrounded the various dishes. As he said to me, "What in h__ do I do now?" I pulled a clean Kleenex from my pocket and retrieved the object and returned it to him.

Getting to understand the extent of hearing difficulties which surround me has helped me realize in a humorous sort of way that I need to be more careful of my enunciation of words. A classic example was when one of the staff members called my new shoes "funky" and I learned on the very first telling that "funky" is *not* a word which you tell to a person who is deaf.

My reason for wanting to use the word was to quote from the newspaper that "Kids of today want a new motto. Instead of 'slow but sure' they have come up with 'fast and funky'."

Of course, we also have several residents who refuse to admit that they have a hearing problem, so they often bluff their way with a nod or a shrug of the shoulders which can either mean that they did not hear you or that they simply don't want to get involved in a discussion.

When telephoning one of the male residents who had quite a coughing spell during the conversation, I said, "Your cough proves that you are allergic to me." His reply was, "Did you say that you are going to put me in a coffin?"

One woman overheard me telling my daughter that I no longer brag quite so much about my pretty hair because I am now surrounded by many "crowns of white hair." The woman's response was, "There was a time when we wore a crown to celebrate our birthday but I don't remember seeing one made of white hair."

I also reported to another woman that someone had referred to my hair as "pretty white tresses" and someone nearby said, "Yes, she surely does have some of the nicest trespasses around."

When the Capitol Area Bell Ringers entertained us, the director called for Mary Jane DeBeer in order to give her a message. One of the male residents rushed to the front of the room because he thought the director had said, "Volunteer."

Occasionally humor backfires, especially when it is supplied by an "attention seeker." One day, as I was reading in the library, I kept hearing a noise from across the table that sounded very much like the sound of a zipper. At first I did not even look up, but after hearing the noise several times, I glance up just in time to see this person deliberately combing his hair with a fine-toothed comb. I remember how we used to make this sound when we were kids but I liked it better when we covered the comb with tissue paper and hummed through it to provide a delightful tune.

New residents sometimes confuse me with Ellen who plays our piano so beautifully and we have a lot of fun with this. Actually, the only similarity is our "crown of white hair" which can be duplicated many times in our village. I tell Ellen that I have no problem with this, if she doesn't.

I seem to get such remarks more than Ellen but it probably is because I get around the dining room more, in my attempts at getting to know more people for my human interest stories. She tells me that no one has accused her of being a writer but I often get asked about my piano playing.

The funniest of these comments came when a resident said to me, "Do you play the piano?" or "Do you play the organ?" When I replied in the negative the resident said, "What do you do that is important?" I was so proud of myself for replying, "Stay on my feet."

During the past two years I have become more and more aware of the constant repetitive questions which reach the staff members at the front desk. The most common one is, "Is the mail in yet?" without even looking to see if the sign is out. Facetiously, I have offered to stand at the desk for one hour for several days in order to answer this question. I offered to do so at a charge of $.05 per question but no one took me up on it.

Once, when our assistant managers were headed for a vacation trip, I presented them with a spray can that dispels a "wrinkle free" mist for clothing. Because I had not explained what the spray was for, the woman immediately put her hands to her face. As the expression goes, "I nearly cracked up" as I realized that the woman must have wondered why I hadn't used it on my *own* face.

Just recently, after observing several complaints at the desk, the substitute receptionist said to me, "I've only been here two hours and I already have a headache." When I replied that I thought I might be getting an ulcer, a resident who was walking by remarked, "Can you get an ulcer in the *head?*"

Touche!!

Unsung Heroes

"He alone is an acute observer who can observe minutely
without being observed."
– Lavater

The people of whom I write within the pages of this chapter will,
indeed, be surprised to see their names in print, for they are among
the many who have been an inspiration for the writing of this book.
Time simply has not permitted any more personal interviews than
have been made, in order to have the book in publication as soon
as possible.

It is extremely important that I recognize those who have served me
well by their attitude, their courtesy and their demeanor as residents
of Independence Village:

Olga Nickels was a friend long before coming to Independence
Village and was my neighbor for several years at Hidden Tree
Apartments (formerly Pine Forest) of East Lansing. She was most
supportive of my earlier writing, especially my first novel and the
book which I have written about the true life story of a young man
(a former college student) who endured the humiliation of false arrest,
conviction and sentencing for a crime which he did *not* commit.

Shortly after arriving at Independence Village I decided to put my
novel, *Samantha Sings Her Song,* on tape so that Olga could hear my
story. Her kindness and patience will always be remembered.
Besides this I marvel at her ability to *always* look her very best
whenever I meet her. She presents to the world a dignified acceptance of impaired eyesight and makes me very proud to claim her as
a special friend.

Mary Jane DeBeer has become a friend through recognition of a
special love which we share with her daughter and husband, Bruce
and Peg Cheney. Bruce was my immediate superior during the years

that we both taught for Michigan State University in the Port Huron area as part of its Elementary Intern Program.

Mary Jane has proven to be the fine person that her family represents her to be and it was part of my karma that we now live within a few doors of each other.

Hubert and Alice Ellison have been very supportive of special programs and events at Independence Village and may possibly be one of the best known couples. Had I done a chapter about them its title would have been either "Mr. and Mrs. Beau Brummel" (because of their fastidious dressing at all times) or "Ambassadors of Good Will" (because they are supportive of so many people).

Vern Kauffman and I have become partners in our appreciation of each other's special talent and have become very supportive with our constructive criticism. I have tremendous respect for Vern's talent and am proud that he keeps me informed of new paintings as he completes them.

He encourages me with sincere comments about my writing, telling me which ones are good, better, or best. In return I tell him what I like best about his paintings, although I do not feel as qualified as I should be for such an assessment. We are most fortunate to have access to Vern's exhibits from time to time.

Gale Owen is one of the calmest and most sincere residents of our Village and I value his opinions at all times. For several months I sat at his table in the dining room where I learned to appreciate his quiet wisdom and subtle humor. Above all, I have never heard an unkind word from his lips.

Hayward Getty has been involved with writing, especially during recent years. Most of it has been in the area of family history and genealogy. Perhaps I also identify with him because his favorite hobbies for many years have been writing and playing bridge. What I have learned most about him is his constant regard for the welfare of other people, particularly those who are his neighbors in our Village.

Aixa Blanco has been one of my most fervent admirers and I deeply appreciate the boost she gives to my ego by telling me that, when she reads our *Village Spotlight News,* the first thing she looks for is my *Brighter Side* monthly column. She often graces our lobby with her cheerful smile and optimistic outlook.

Helen Mutch has very generously devoted her time to greeting newcomers and helping them feel at home. We have had many talks and seem to have a great deal in common with similar backgrounds of Pharmacy within our families.

Walter Smith and Alice Franke have been an inspiration because of the way in which they always have a cheerful word for others and do not pass judgement on what other residents do. It is a real *joy* to have them around and I often take the route to my second floor apartment via the pool table area, simply because they add a cheerfulness to my day.

Florence Storm is an encouraging person to meet and to know because of her determination to do all that she can to remain active. She also has a dry sense of humor that amuses me, especially when I realize there is a touch of wisdom behind it.

Esther Eyle has often been an encouragement to me by including me in her select group of friends and by sharing her family with me. She *is,* however, hard on my pocket book because she keeps me informed about special clothing and jewelry sales!

Beryl Woodman has added a special dignity to our Village, in an unassuming way. In fact, she will be surprised to learn how much she has influenced my life. She has a very quiet and unpretentious manner which speaks of wisdom but she does not go unnoticed because of her diminutive and stylish posture.

Paul and Katharyn Sweet caught my attention on the very first day of their arrival, mostly because they seem to be such a "together" couple – with a smile and a kind word for everyone they meet. They surely are rightfully named and I enjoy calling them "The Sweets" of our Village.

Clarence "Clancy" Vinge is no longer a resident of Independence Village and I miss our interesting short talks. Perhaps the fact that we both taught at Michigan State University has created a bond which allowed us to talk "issues" from time to time. After moving to Great Lakes Homes in Holt, Michigan, he mailed me postage for sending copies of my articles which get published. I consider this a very fine compliment.

Mary Pollack has become a very special friend, especially since moving to her table in the dining room. I have sometimes been amazed at how well we communicate. She has a very special way of feeding my ego with her compliments about my choice of clothing and jewelry. Mary has endeared herself to the hearts of many people and several of them stop at our table daily to call her "Sweetheart." Mary is ninety-five years of age with a sharp mind!

Members of the Wheelchair Brigade have been an inspiration and have taught me true compassion as I see them facing life in an accepting way. Almost without exception, they display a patience from which we could all learn. Even being run over by the wheels of one of the wheelchairs, shortly after breaking a toe, has not diminished my belief that these special people deserve our compassion but *not* our pity. With them, their dignity truly is the "name of the game."

Members of the Entire Staff at Independence Village have earned my gratitude for their unselfish services and their determination to provide a healthy, happy atmosphere for each and every one of us!

Are You Somebody's Grandma?

During an Easter weekend I chose to find a comfortable spot in one of my favorite malls where I could enjoy my favorite pastime of "people watching."

As usual, I found a convenient bench for sitting and was almost immediately rewarded by the sudden appearance of a "well endowed" woman (fiftyish) who, literally, plopped herself down at the opposite end of my bench – with an audible sigh of relief.

Holding onto her hand was one of the most adorable little boys I ever hope to meet. In fact, he was so full of vim and zip that it didn't take long to figure out why the woman was so weary.

Although I have very acute hearing, I could only guess at what the boy had whispered into the woman's ear. She gave me a faint clue when she said aloud, "Why don't you ask her?'

In the way that children so often do, he "inched" his way until he touched my knee and offered me an almost angelic smile. Without hesitation, and as I smiled back at him, he asked, "Are you somebody's Grandma?" When I replied that I am, he surprised me by saying, "Then you must like to read." What an unasked-for tribute to grandmothers!

As he pulled a coloring book from behind his back for me to see and asked, "Could you read me some of these stories?" I breathed a sigh of relief that it was a Mother Goose book. Only a few of the pages were enriched with words which I read to him as he nestled beside me so that he could see the words as I saw them – straight on.

Later, as we encountered nursery rhyme pictures without words, I told the story as best I could remember it. Fortunately, for me, the only rhymes he wanted repeated were the pages with words.

During the "getting acquainted" time with the boy I noticed a young couple who approached and sat down on the bench across from us. The man was Caucasian and the woman was of Asian decent. It was not until then that I realized the boy was Vietnamese and that the older woman was the paternal grandmother because the man looked just like her – same eyes, same nose and same ingratiating smile.

Both parents indicated with gestures and smiles that told me that they appreciated my taking over the responsibility of entertaining their son. In fact, as they made their departure a few minutes later, the man whispered in my ear, "What would you charge for teaching our "Tony" until he is ready for Kindergarten in about six months?"

Little did he know that I am a retired teacher of reading, both with children and adults, so I felt a special glow that so many of my communications skills apparently were very much alive after ten years of retirement. Yet, what pleased me most was the fact that I had learned *so much* about attitudes, thought processes and the keen curiosity of this boy in such a short period of time.

As I started to talk to "Tony" about Cinderella and her step-sisters he interrupted me to say, "Oh, I know all about them and I *hate* that ugly grandmother!"

I fully expected him to ask what a "godmother" is when he babbled something about how she probably got that funny name because she was not nice like *his* mommy and grandma. At that moment, the woman at the end of our bench turned to us with a big grin.

When I said to him, "Oh, is this your grandma?" He replied, "Sure, can't you tell she belongs to *me?*

As we turned to another page in the book I, literally, prayed that he would not ask me to tell him the story about *Rumplestiltskin* because it was one of the wordless pages and my mind drew a complete blank!

Actually, he saved me just in time by saying, "Oh, well, let's forget about it 'cause I can't 'pernounce' it anyway." It almost seemed like he sensed my discomfort and wanted to comfort me. Children have an almost uncanny sense of such things.

Just to change the pace a bit, I made use of the opportunity to "hone my skills" by asking such things as, "Do you supposed you can find a page to color that is just like the picture on the cover?" His answer was, "Oh, sure, but I will have to peek at the cover when I can't 'member' the colors." How happy I was that, at no time, did I correct his pronunciation for truly this was "Tony's language."

Even later, I smiled as I asked him how he had learned so *much* before he is even in Kindergarten and he informed me that he was four and one-half years old and was in "mersery" school.

Noticing that he asked me three times to read him the rhyme about *Old Mother Hubbard* I said, "You really like that story, don't you?" His answer was, "Yup, I *do,* but I'm worried about it." Without my needing to say a word about why he was worried he said, "I just keep wondering if that old lady *ever* found her dog a bone!" Just as I was hoping to offer some reassurance, but on a child's level, his parents indicated that it was time to leave.

After folding up his coloring book and hopping down from our special bench he grinned and said, "Can I kiss you good-bye?" When I replied, "How about a big *hug?*" he jumped back onto the bench and gave me a bear hug that I will never forget!

Once again, I was reminded of how glad I was that I had carried a note pad and pen for jotting down what I did not want to forget about this "strange encounter." It pleased me, also, to recall how many times in my life I have served as a surrogate grandmother or mother to children – and sometimes to adults.

In just a few minutes of time I had learned more about the brightness of this little boy than any IQ test would ever tell me.

My Story
Part One

My story about the ambition which still possesses me in this 78th year of life has sent me searching for just *one* experience which has, perhaps, taught me more about "stick-to-it-iveness" than any other that I can remember.

Because so many have asked me how long I have felt that my writing is worth doing I would have to say that it all revolves around the feeling that each of us is on this earth to make the very best of what life has dealt us. I am just as certain that people do not really want to hear about our mishaps and discouragements. They simply want to know what makes us the happiest.

In 1937 I was selected to serve as County School Commissioner for the residents of Monroe County, Michigan, and it was both a traumatic experience and full-filling one. From the word *"go"* I was constantly aware that I needed to prove myself worthy of this honor. It was not always easy but it was never *dull.*

It was at this time that I made the decision that *nothing* would stand in the way of success for even a fleeting moment.

I was twenty-two years of age at the time and I knew only too well that I received the appointment mostly because I rode into it on my dad's shirt tails. He was actually involved in politics and simply knew that he had the necessary votes in his hip pocket.

I have never understood why he chose *me* for this almost insurmountable hurdle but I learned very early in the term of office that it was expected of me to succeed. Just as I knew in Kindergarten that I was expected to go to college. I have much respect for anyone who understands what is expected of him and heads for that course.

I have even more respect for the person who sees beyond his environmental restrictions with a drive that makes him succeed, "in spite of Hell or high water!" I have met people like this in all walks of life and they have made me proud to be their friend.

As I campaigned for the school commissioner's job I soon learned that when I could look at difficult situations with a sense of humor I was much more inclined to succeed.

Perhaps the funniest of those campaigning experiences happened when I had to, literally, climb a fence in order to reach the farmhouse of one of the voting county supervisors. All dressed up in a beautiful white linen suit I slipped and landed in "you know what." Only the loving words of a beloved brother helped me realize that, if I could maintain my dignity, I probably could contribute this experience as my finest lesson in *composure.*"

I remember that there were thirteen candidates for this interim position and that it required thirteen times of vote casting before I was the one selected.

Throughout the final day of voting I never once felt that I was that much more qualified than any of the other candidates. All that I really had going for me, other than my father's political clout, was that I had had as much formal education and teaching experience, plus the knowledge that, throughout my twenty-two years, I had learned to never back away from something which I wanted so much for my own self-esteem. And, of course, I needed to become the person that my father expected me to be.

As the result of the final vote was reported and my victory was announced I looked around the crowded room and nearly panicked because I could not see the face of my father! He had slipped out to his car to return with two boxes of cigars to pass out to the crowd, composed mostly of *men.*

I still remember my chagrin as I burst into tears when making my acceptance speech and being told, later, that it might have been one of my "greatest moves" in the political arena.

On a very small scale it was also the beginning of the realization that politics was not for *me.* Being required to shake hands with people for whom I had little respect; kissing drooling babies with dirt-smeared faces; eating meals of wild game with other politicians as we visited what was then called the "county poor house" or "county farm" and uttering words of congratulations at times when I really did not mean them placed a heavy burden of self-guilt which I knew I had to shake.

At the end of the two years of interim service my convictions were strong enough to persuade me to *not* seek reelection – though, by then, I was certain that I could win.

I felt no sadness because of my decision because, by that time, I had decided that it was time for my beloved Mac and me to raise a family. This was the excuse that my dad gave to people who asked why I was "quitting politics" so it was actually funny that our first child was not born until 18 months later.

The strength of character which I inherited from *both* of my parents continues to guide my life as I refuse to give up in my attempts to become a good writer.

No one wants to hear what a struggle this has been for many years but they *do* need to know that I shall never give up in my attempts to be well accepted in the publishing arena.

How I wish that everyone I meet could arise every morning with the feeling that there is still work to be done, simply because I have made that promise to myself.

My freelance writing is at its peak, especially since having more time for it while living in Independence Village in East Lansing. It no longer is just because I came here expecting to *live* my life to its fullest. Nor that there is a sense of security and love all around me. In fact, it has become almost a selfish obsession as I realize that it is here that I am constantly finding more to write about than time will probably allow.

I continue to keep in contact with many people outside the village, with an emphasis on young people, but never excluding my peers. My strongest advice is for everyone to make new friends but to cherish the old. If one does not do so he will find himself as an isolated old person with no goal.

We must all have something to look forward to each day, even if it is only that we can make another happy simply by being nearby.

Along the roadway for my writing I have felt a certain destiny that I have something worth saying, so I talk to my word processor day and night as the spirit moves me. I also realize that this is never accomplished by oneself, alone. Experience has taught me that I have been blessed with a very special "angel on my shoulder." She encourages me and she scolds me – but always she *loves* me.

My favorite maxim about writing is that "To write well is at once to think well, to feel rightly, and to render properly. It is to have, at the same time, mind, soul, taste." – *Ovid*

I have, indeed, been blessed by the presence of good thinkers all around me. If they happen to have a delightful sense of humor – all the better. So long as this continues to happen for *me* I shall continue to be *rich.* I no longer have the time of day for unkind acts and this is one of my reasons for selecting a retirement village where I can "sort the men from the boys" and the "good-doers from the do-gooders."

There is so much talent all around me that the source for my stories is endless, all of which are based on tremendous courage of the people whom I meet on a daily basis.

It is now that I realize what Shakespeare meant when he wrote:

"Love all, trust a few. Do wrong to none; be able to thine enemy rather in power than in use; and keep thine friend under thine own life's key. Be checked for silence, but never taxed for speech."

My Story
Part Two

It is virtually impossible for me to look at the freshness of a new day, particularly a sunny one, and not feel that it has promise of some sort. Even the most discouraged would have to realize this just a little.

Unless one has experienced the utter loneliness of being a "fifth wheel" one cannot have true compassion or even empathy for the feeling. "Whistling in the dark" can become an empty tune unless one can come to terms with why he is doing it. Only then can it become therapeutic release as one learns to become more concerned for others than for oneself. Then, before long, there comes peace.

Just as a palm tree sheds its coconuts when they become full-grown, so must an individual shed his troubles. Fond memories help more than any prescription drug and I feel certain that it is God's will that helps us bury our heartaches.

One of my greatest faults has been that I sometimes talk too much, which has brought forth all sorts of criticism – most of it with a touch of humor.

Even as I write this story I chuckle as I recall being touched by this while walking in the mall with one of my favorite relatives. As I gabbed with his wife he left us, only to return to place in my hand a miniature trophy with the inscribed words, "Yackety-Yack."

This may have been the beginning of learning to laugh at myself, which is a very healthy sign.

I recall another incident (many years ago) when my husband showed me a fifty-dollar bill and informed me that, if I could refrain from talking for forty-eight hours, I could keep the money. I felt certain that I could manage such a feat since we would be at our respective jobs or sleeping about thirty of those hours.

Much to my surprise, as I was preparing dinner at the forty-sixth hour, Mac walked into the room, handed me the fifty-dollar bill and said, "For God's sake, *talk.*"

One learns early in a good marriage that no price is too much to pay to retain that happiness! Because of my man's confidence in me it would be an insult to him for me to not remember that life is for the living.

As we look around at the sadness and evil that surrounds us we sometimes see evidence of carelessness and irresponsibility which seems to exist wherever we go.

As retirees, we try to make amends by being supportive of worthy causes within our financial and physical means. Most of all, we live for *today* and do our best to not mourn for a past that we can never bring back nor a future which carries no definite promise.

Because I want to provide a fair assessment, I have now visited with residents from several retirement homes and have decided that there are similarities so obvious that the choice of one becomes an extremely personal one. Usually, location, pleasant surroundings and availability to health services become the key factors in the final decision.

I have talked with a few residents outside the Lansing area also, and their stories are much like the ones which I am getting in Independence Village.

One close friend has even reminded me that living in a retirement center is not for *everyone.* It merely becomes a viable choice worth considering.

Because I have been widowed for twenty-two years, some of my difficult decisions have probably been easier to handle because I got an early start. My changes in retirement life style have gone from a large country home to a ranch home in Okemos and to a series of apartments in the Lansing area. So my "worldly possessions" have been dispersed gradually.

This must be easier than giving up so *much* in "one fell swoop!"

My editor has almost insisted that it is time for me to tell of a series of scary incidents which finally prompted me to make the decision to move to a retirement community. Some of this will even come as a surprise to my family because, at the time, I felt that it was not necessary to cause them any more concern than they already had.

We are an extremely close family and I began, a few years ago considering possibilities of how I could best free them of unnecessary worry.

Among the experiences which most influenced my decision to move to Independence Village were being followed home by another automobile several times; having my car windows shot at by teenagers with pellet guns; being affronted while stopping for a red light by a tap on my car window and a request for money; having a gold necklace grabbed from my neck while shopping; and being the victim of an attempted mugging!

All of these incidents took place when I was not in my apartment but I recall how very frightened I was because I had to return to my home alone. Since living in a retirement village, there has always been the wonderful feeling of returning to a place of security and where other residents really *care!*

I even have a slight suspicion that it was my son-in-law who was "conned" into making the suggestive request, "Have you ever thought of looking into a retirement community situation, Mother?" My only reason for thinking this is that it is sometimes easier when the suggestion does not need to come from a son or daughter.

The final "punch line" for this book has arrived from an out-of-town physician who has written, "Thank you for your newspaper article about living in Independence Village. I am not yet ready to make such a decision but it is nice to know that there are such choices. I only wish I had known this in time to assist my mother. Keep up the good work!"